Pub Pews

Cheryl A. Buettin

TRILOGY CHRISTIAN PUBLISHERS
TUSTIN, CA

Trilogy Christian Publishers
A Wholly Owned Subsidary of Trinity Broadcasting Network
2442 Michelle Drive
Tustin, CA 92780

Cover photo by Robert Czerniak.

Rights Department, 2442 Michelle Drive, Tustin, CA 92780.

Trilogy Christian Publishing/TBN and colophon are trademarks of Trinity Broadcasting Network.

For information about special discounts for bulk purchases, please contact Trilogy Christian Publishing.

Trilogy Disclaimer: The views and content expressed in this book are those of the author and may not necessarily reflect the views and doctrine of Trilogy Christian Publishing or the Trinity Broadcasting Network.

10 9 8 7 6 5 4 3 2 1

Library of Congress Cataloging-in-Publication Data is available.
ISBN 978-1-64773-584-5
ISBN 978-1-64773-585-2 (ebook)

Contents

Prologue

Verona, whose slogan is "More Than a Dot—It Is a Spot," is a small borough located thirteen miles northeast of downtown Pittsburgh. It faces the deciduous Allegheny Mountain Range and is nestled on the left bank of the Allegheny River, one of the three rivers dissecting Pittsburgh, Pennsylvania.

It was once a thriving spot, indeed. It had been a railroad stop with many shops lining the downtown area. It once had lumberyards, a steel casting plant, a chemical plant, Wooding-Verona Toolworks, and the Daily juice factory, a cocktail mix and juice jug production plant that still exists. Most everyone in Verona's heyday worked. It was a quaint, blue-collar community where doors were always unlocked, kids ran around the streets and played in each other's backyards, and fellowship amongst neighbors was a daily occurrence. But the tides changed for this small "spot" town when many of the factories closed in the eighties. The final straw was when Edgewater Steel, which employed much of Verona's citizens, closed in 2001.

The demographics of Verona are now made up of many divorced, single moms, where the median age is under thirty and there are a minority of people with disabilities, because of Verona's low and affordable rent. The last street surrounded by the six square blocks of residential properties is a street called Arch Street, located directly on the banks of the Allegheny River. On Arch Street are the Allegheny River Pub, a VFW club, and at the dead end, by lock number three, the First Baptist Church of Verona.

Inside the Allegheny River Pub sat Lizzy Murphy, cleaning the deep fryer, which, in her mind, was the most disgusting, repulsive job in the world, but it had to be done every Sunday, the day the pub was closed. Lizzy was the third-generation owner of the pub located in Verona. There wasn't a day that had gone by in the last twelve years that she hadn't said to herself, "Why am I here, and how am I going to get out of here? Even more important, whatever possessed me to make that promise to my dad?"

CHAPTER 1

Lizzy finished scraping the last bit of blackish-brown, malodorous sludge into the trash before putting the fryer pans into the degreaser in the sink to soak. She was going to get a soda from behind the bar, when she heard a loud knock at the side entrance to the pub. A clean-cut man of about thirty stood at the glass door. She had never met him before. He waved for her to come toward the door. She went into the entry and talked through the glass.

"What do you want?" As a single female pub owner, she had become guarded and edgy.

"I am sorry to bother you. I am the pastor at the First Baptist Church down the street, and I really need to talk to you," the man said with a warm smile.

He seemed legitimate, so Lizzy took a deep breath, unlocked the door, and let him in. He stepped into the entry.

"What's up?" She didn't really want to make eye contact with him because she felt like a mess and was sure she smelt like burnt fryer oil.

He said in a somewhat anxious voice, "My name is Brad Schmidt, and as I said, I am the pastor from down the street. The church had a fire in the middle of the night. Thankfully, no one was hurt, but there's been quite a bit of damage. If it hadn't been for the sprinkler system, it might have been worse." He paused. "Someone who attends the church said that you have a large, empty garage, and I was wondering if the church could rent the garage from you and put our seventy pews in there. It would mean so much to our congregation to have our services there while we repair the sanctuary, possibly for a couple of months because of the water damage." After a longer pause, Brad asked, "If you agree, do you think we could set the pews up for a service tonight at six o'clock, since you won't be open?"

Lizzy didn't take long to think about his request because she certainly needed the extra money. The garage was separated from the bar by a wall and the door to the kitchen, which could be locked. It had its own entrance from the parking lot. The two-story dock door could open to easily bring in the pews. Moreover, she didn't have any plans for the night and would be available if there was a problem.

She said to Brad, "I think that would work, but perhaps you should look at the garage before we make any formal arrangements." She led him through the pub, and the kitchen and through the door. The garage was mostly empty, except for some cleaning supplies by the kitchen door and several banquet tables that leaned against the wall next to the supplies. It was clean and large enough to fit three semi-trucks inside. Lizzy couldn't be sure, but she figured it would provide ample room enough to place the seventy pews in rows.

After looking at the garage, Brad's elated eyes lit up. "What do you think would be a fair price to rent this space?"

Lizzy had no idea what to charge. She was excited to be getting any money at this point. She replied, "Would fifty dollars a week be alright? You can take the space as long as you want. I don't have any plans for it anyway."

Brad gave it some thought. "I was thinking more like a hundred, but under the circumstances, why don't we split the difference and make it seventy-five dollars a week? And both the church and I would truly appreciate it."

They were shaking hands when another loud knock came from the entry door. As they made their way back to the front door, Lizzy recognized the woman standing outside as one of the local news reporters from KDKA News, Pittsburgh. Behind her stood a cameraman. The news reporter asked, "Are you Brad Schmidt? Someone at the church said we would find you here. We have some questions about the fire at your church."

"Yes, but let's go down at the church and let this young lady go back to work."

Lizzy felt flattered that he thought she was young, because at the moment she certainly didn't feel that way.

He turned to Lizzy. "Would it be alright to bring the pews over at noon?"

"Sure, that would be fine." She knew she would still be there at noon, finishing cleaning the pub and preparing for opening on Monday. Lizzy let Brad out. Brad had walked over, so the news crew and Brad got inside the KDKA van and drove toward the church on Arch Street.

Ten minutes before noon, Lizzy went downstairs. She had taken a shower, still feeling embarrassed about her earlier appearance and for having smelt like burnt grease. She'd put on a nice sweater and jeans, along with some makeup, trying to cover her freckles, then she pulled her hair into her usual ponytail. She looked outside and noticed the snow was falling at a steady pace now. It wasn't unusual to have snow in March in Pittsburgh. In fact, one of the worst snowstorms took place on Saint Patrick's Day 1993; the city had shut down when almost twenty-four inches fell in twenty-four hours. Just as she opened the doors, a red pickup truck pulled into the parking lot. She could see there were four men in the cab of the truck. The bed of the truck was stacked with the pews. Lizzy thought they must be making several trips because she knew for sure that there weren't seventy pews in the back of that pickup truck.

Lizzy waved and yelled to them, "Back into the garage, it will be easier." She marshaled them like she was directing a plane, using hand signals as they backed into the garage.

Brad noticed how nice Lizzy looked cleaned up, how attractive she was, and her vivacious mannerism. He was also impressed by how skilled and in command she seemed. He waved at her through the open window and yelled, "Thanks."

The four men all got out of the four-door cab, and Brad made quick introductions. She noticed that they had brought a stack of towels, she was guessing to wipe the snow off the pews after they arrived.

"It's all yours. Go ahead and place them wherever you want." Then she jokingly said, "Mi casa es su casa," and turned toward the kitchen door. "I'll be in the kitchen preparing food for tomorrow. I will leave the kitchen door open if you need anything."

"Thanks again for everything. I am serious when I say you really came to the rescue. I wasn't sure what I would have done if you had said no." Then he turned to go help the others by directing the setup and positioning of the pews.

Lizzy suddenly realized Brad was a fairly good-looking man. She would have noticed that before if she had bothered to look at his face when she first met him. He had a chiseled chin, light flawless completion, wavy blond hair, and big blue eyes. There was something inviting about his smile; his teeth were ultra-white, straight, and surrounded by soft, well-defined lips. He was tall and thin, but not lanky.

Lizzy went into the kitchen and said to herself, "Monday meat loaf, and the soup of the day will be chicken noodle soup. Better get started." She walked into the kitchen and set to work preparing the next day's specials.

Lizzy stuck with Grandma and Mom's traditional blue plate daily specials, which consisted of a meat—such as meat loaf, fried chicken, beef stew, or fried fish; a starch—like a potato; and a vegetable. The daily special would be posted on an erase board on the wall by the kitchen. Along with the daily specials, most of the food sold was fried wings, French fries, fried jalapeño poppers, fried mozzarella sticks, and fried zucchini. Lizzy would refer to them as "pub food," which was delivered by Sysco Food Services. She used to place orders with Sysco once a week. Now she placed an order with them once a month, a true reflection of how sluggish business was. If it wasn't for the liquor sales, she thought to herself, the pub wouldn't survive.

Deep in Lizzy's heart, she didn't like the alcohol part of the business. She didn't drink herself, and she didn't particularly like being around people who drank in excess. They seemed loud and obnoxious, and she felt like she might be contributing to an addiction. She wished the pub was more of a food business. In fact, her dream was to convert the pub into a wedding reception venue. She would visualize the delicious food, and the beautifully decorated cakes, but most of all, how beautiful the wedding pictures would look with the river and mountains as the backdrop. Really, Lizzy was a clean-cut, hopeful romantic at heart, so becoming a bar owner was not what she was passionate about. However, she knew the wedding reception idea was just a dream, and the possibility of it actually happening dropped as each year passed by.

Brad lightly knocked on the kitchen door, not wanting to startle Lizzy. Lizzy was putting away the last clean cutting board. "We are done in the garage, and the others have headed back. I wanted to thank you again. Here's the check for this week."

Lizzy was curious. "May I look at what you have done?"

"Sure. It's your place, you can do whatever you want." He chuckled. "Come on out and take a look for yourself."

When she walked into the garage, Lizzy was amazed. It truly looked like a church except for the stark concrete floors and walls. "Wow, what a transformation. Those pews are beautiful. Where did you get them?" The pews were indeed beautiful. They were solid oak with exquisitely hand-carved ends.

"It's an interesting story I don't mind sharing with you. I already have my sermon that was supposed to be given this morning, so I am free for a while."

Lizzy thought how interesting it was that he would have any time, considering his church had had a fire that night. "Just let me close up and lock the garage. We can go sit inside the pub to talk. Do you want a drink?" She softly laughed. "A soft drink, of course."

He gave out a hearty laugh of his own. "That would be great. It's about time I get to know my neighbor," he said with a smile. Brad and Lizzy only lived less than a quarter of a mile apart, but they ran in different circles, and if it hadn't been for the fire, they might never have met.

They walked through the kitchen and into the pub. Lizzy flipped on the lights. "Make yourself at home." Brad pulled out a bar stool and sat down.

"Do you prefer Coke or Sprite?"

"I prefer Sprite. Thanks"

While Lizzy was pouring the drinks, Brad looked around. He thought the pub looked rustic and inviting. There were ten round tables and chairs, with napkins and condiments situated in the center of each table. There was also a pool table, dartboard, and big-screen TV against the far wall. What really impressed him were the glass sliders facing the river and mountains. He had never seen a deck that big before. It had eight covered, round outdoor patio tables and chairs, now blanketed with snow. He couldn't believe he had never come in here before, but quite honestly, he had felt like it wasn't a good idea. If someone from the church saw him go into a pub, it could get the church's rumor mill started. He couldn't afford to tarnish his reputation while he was trying to grow the church. He thought to himself that was probably a ridiculous reason for not coming over to meet Lizzy and made a mental note to get out to meet more of the neighbors.

Lizzy delivered the drinks and sat next to him. Because the bar stools swiveled, they could face each other as they talked. Normally, Lizzy stayed behind the bar, where her comfort zone was. Today, though, she wasn't sure why, but she felt confident enough to come to the other side. She immediately started with a question. Dad would always tell her, 'It's better to listen than to tell, especially in this business.' She asked, "How did someone so young become a pastor, and where did you get those beautiful pews?"

Brad grinned. "Thank you for the compliment, but actually I am thirty-five years old. And the pews, as I said, are an interesting story." He took a deep breath and said, "I am a third-generation preacher. My grandfather was the pastor of the Emmanuel Lutheran Church, which is still there on Allegheny River Boulevard." When Lizzy nodded, Brad continued, "My dad must have been rebellious because he decided to go to a Baptist seminary instead. When he graduated from college, the Southern Baptist Convention had just purchased the old Allegheny Rowing Club, where the church sits now, and they offered my dad the position to start a new congregation. This meant a total renovation of the old rowing club. He was very young and had to hire help to gut the place and add a steeple to the building. He felt tremendous pressure to keep the costs down. Apparently, that is when my grandfather came to his rescue. He hooked Dad up with a Lutheran church downtown, in the 'Deutschtown' district, that was getting rid of their pews to replace them with cushioned seating. Dad always said he felt like he'd had a second miracle getting those pews—because I was his first miracle. You can see the beautiful workmanship of the pews, which were made by the Amish people over in Lancaster, Pennsylvania. The pews are over one hundred and fifty years old, but apparently Dad got them for, as he said, 'a prayer and a song.'"

"You are right, that is an interesting story." Lizzy then asked, "So, where are your mom and dad now?"

"I took over the church from Dad when he moved to a church in Nashville, Tennessee, the same year Mom died from breast cancer. I don't think he could stand the memories. I was only twenty-five, but I had already been the youth pastor at the Baptist church for four years. That was in 2009. I go to visit Dad in Nashville, or he sometimes comes here. We try to get together at least twice a year. I think he still misses Mom to this day. He never had the desire to replace her, and he has never remarried. I miss her, too. She was such an energetic and loving person...

"So, what is your story? How did someone so young get to be the owner of a pub? And what about *your* parents?"

Lizzy gave a nervous laugh, knowing her dad would not have approved, but started to tell her story anyway. "Unfortunately, my mom died in 2001 from a heart attack, and my dad died the following year of pneumonia. Years before, Grandpa Al and Grandma JoJo Murphy bought this building, which used to be a tool shop, to fulfill their dream of owning a pub. They always called it 'a place where good food, libations, and conversations would gather'—like they remembered pubs to be like back in Ireland. That was in 1961. My dad, Patrick, was just sixteen years old.

"I remember hearing the stories. How they would laugh about the 'Irish luck' they had when acquiring all the equipment for the bar and restaurant. They got it all from a closed business called 'The Ducky.' Grandpa Al and Dad would say, 'We practically stole the equipment,' and they would call the closed restaurant 'the Unlucky Ducky.'"

Lizzy smiled a moment, realizing the coincidence, then said, "I guess we have that in common. Our dads got such good deals they both felt they got lucky." They both laughed in agreement.

Lizzy concluded, "The grand opening of the Allegheny River Pub was held during the Christmas holidays of '61. When it opened, the whole community was there in excitement and support of Grandpa, Grandma, and Dad. There was a snowstorm that night, the snow falling on the lit thirty-foot Christmas tree they had placed on the deck outside the back glass doors. They always described it, 'a dream come true,' 'a magical day,' and 'a day to always remember.'"

With that, Brad stood up. "Wow, I think your story is much more interesting than mine, and I think you are a much better storyteller, too." He chuckled and thought to himself that Lizzy was enthusiastically well-spoken.

He turned to walk out, but then turned back around. "Would you like to come to tonight's service?"

Lizzy hesitated. Her parents had been known in the area for their abundant generosity and acts of kindness. But even though her family were good people, they were not churchgoers. More out of curiosity than anything else, Lizzy found herself saying "yes." She added jokingly, "After all, I only have to walk down the steps to get there because I live above the pub."

Brad laughed. "Great. See you at six. Don't wear yourself out walking down those stairs." He walked out the door.

Lizzy laughed to herself after Brad left. He was not only handsome but also funny. He was the type of guy she liked. *But who knows? He's thirty-five. He probably was married before.* Lizzy hadn't seen a wedding ring, but she figured he could have taken it off while moving the pews. With a long sigh, she thought, *Enough of that, Lizzy Murphy. Get back to work.*

CHAPTER 2

Lizzy finished the last of her preparations for Monday and decided to grab a soda. She sat down at the bar, looked up, and saw the family crest, with the words "Murphy's Pub, established 1961" below it. Apparently talking to Brad had stirred up memories from the past. She thought about herself and her sister Vickie's early years, how she was mostly under the care of Vickie while Mom and Dad worked downstairs at the pub. Mom would come upstairs to bring them meals and check in from time to time. Lizzy never thought it was abnormal to live above a pub. Those were happy times. She and Vickie were always very close, entertaining each other while their parents worked. But the age difference of five years eventually became a nemesis, and Vickie became bossy, even more so when Lizzy was with her friends.

As they grew older, Lizzy started to look more like their mom. She was five-foot-two and in a constant battle with her weight. She would have been described as 'cute.' She had good features and a beautiful complexion, with robin's-egg speckled freckles across her nose and cheeks. She had big, expressive brown eyes and long, straight light brown hair, like Mom, which she would always pull back into a ponytail. She also had a pretty smile. Her personality was 'spunky' like her mom's, too. Vickie, on the other hand, looked more like Dad, who was described as 'devastatingly' handsome, tall, and athletic. He had blue eyes and jet-black hair. Vickie grew to become a female version of Dad. She had curly jet-black hair and blue eyes, and she was tall and slender. She looked like a model in any magazine.

So, it was no surprise to anyone that when Lizzy was in seventh grade, Vickie went off to college, and soon after she met and fell in love with a good-looking medical student and got married. Vickie and her husband moved to Bucks County, near Philadelphia, and bought an estate with horses while he started a successful cardiology practice. They eventually had two children, a boy named Colin and a girl named Katherine. They were Lizzy's nephew and niece, but she had no relationship with them and barely knew them. Lizzy and Vickie had drifted so far apart that Lizzy thought they might as well be on different planets. They rarely spoke to each other, probably because Lizzy felt envious and jealous because Vickie had gotten what she wanted. Vickie never reached out to Lizzy, either. She never called to see how she was or how the pub was doing. Either way, the silence wasn't always bliss.

The pub started doing so well that Dad decided to build a marina. In 1995—the same year Vickie got married—he took out a large loan and built a sixty-five-slip marina. It was quite the undertaking: a floating barge, anchored and pounded with a huge crane in huge metal pylons. Lizzy remembered it making a thunderous sound as they lowered the boom on the pylon. There were constant hammering sounds as the wood planks turned into walkways and dock slips. Lizzy remembered feeling amazed as she watched the construction, which took most of that summer, with the opening scheduled for the following year. But disaster happened early in 1996, when torrential rains came, flooding the Plum River and pouring large trees and debris into the river. The Allegheny River itself became a raging force. Barges broke loose and took out Oakmont's Yacht Club. Entire docks with boats attached broke off, and everything was swept down the river and deposited into the Ohio River—including Dad's brand-new marina.

That was when the tides changed. With a big loan over their heads, Lizzy had to work hard all through high school. Despite the work, she graduated from high school in the spring of 2001 with honors, and received a scholarship to West Virginia University in the fall. Lizzy was worried and thought Mom and Dad were showing signs of stress. Business had slowed to a snail's pace, and the last straw took place when Edgewater Steel officially closed its doors.

Lizzy reluctantly went off to WVU that fall. Halfway through her first semester she got the dreaded call from Dad that Mom had suffered a major heart attack and had died on the way to the hospital. Lizzy returned home immediately, not knowing that was the last time she would attend college. Her dad needed her more than ever. They went back to WVU to collect her things, and she never stepped on the campus again. Thus ended her dream of becoming a veterinarian.

Dad transferred everything into Lizzy's name the year Mom died, as though he had a premonition. Sure enough, early in 2002, Dad died from complications of pneumonia. Lizzy convinced herself he really died from a broken heart.

So, at the young age of nineteen, she found herself the sole proprietor of the Allegheny River Pub. For the most part, it wasn't so bad, but there were days that seemed to last forever. Now, after twelve years of running the pub, at age thirty-one, she had grown weary. She felt like she was on a hamster wheel with no light at the end of the tunnel. After all, the pub was her mom and dad's dream, not hers. If only she hadn't promised her dad she would take it over, but she'd wanted him to die in peace. As she saw him in the hospital bed gasping for every breath, she made that dreaded statement: "I'd be happy to take over the pub if something happens to you. But that's not going to happen." But it did happen. Her father died later that night while Lizzy was asleep in a chair by his bed.

When the economy failed, property values collapsed, and the pub's loan was valued at more than its worth. She figured in ten years, perhaps, the value would be high enough again to sell it. The thought of ten more years in the pub, though, made her feel hopeless and depressed. She felt stuck, like a truck in mud.

Time went by quickly while she was daydreaming, and now it was past five o'clock. Lizzy ran upstairs to freshen her makeup and brush her teeth before she went down to unlock the garage door and turn on the overhead lights.

It was 5:45 when Brad walked in. "Wow, you are on top of things. I came early to make sure we were all set." He continued, "I am not sure how many are coming because of the confusion that the fire created. If I had to guess, I think it will be less than forty people."

"That's fine," she said, then asked, "How many people attend your church?"

"There are a hundred members, but attendance is usually three-quarters of that." He added, "I am trying to grow the membership, but it's been sluggish. I am not sure if that's a sign of the times, or because, as you know, we are located off the beaten path."

Lizzy agreed to them being off the beaten path, but she had no idea about it being a sign of the times, except for the fact that business for her was sluggish, as well.

Worshipers started to arrive, and surprisingly Brad introduced Lizzy to everyone who entered. He described her as an "earth angel" for supplying a place for them to congregate. Lizzy felt a little embarrassed but also good, since she hadn't heard a compliment about herself in a long time.

Lizzy sat in the back and counted only thirty people at the service, with most sitting up near the front. To Lizzy, it seemed like an excessive number of pews for such a small gathering. Right after it was scheduled to start, a young man went to the front with his guitar and sang the song "How Great Is Our God." Lizzy was very touched by the words and the beautiful, strong voice of the young man.

Then Brad got up and proceeded to the front. Lizzy couldn't help but notice how eloquently he spoke and the ease with which he said an opening prayer. He then asked everyone to turn to Galatians 5:22. Lizzy watched the people flipping through their Bibles until it looked like they hit a dead end and stopped flipping. She didn't have a clue where those people had turned to in the Bible or who the Galatians were. In her mind, it sounded like they were giants—she thought she'd heard there were giants in the Bible somewhere, but she wasn't really sure.

Brad started his sermon after taking a deep breath. "Paul wrote this to the church in Galatia, in today's Turkey. He told the church that they should put away their flesh, their sinful nature, and live in a godly spirit, to inherit the kingdom of God." Then he read the actual scripture from Galatians 5:22: "'But the fruit of the Spirit is love, joy, peace, patience, kindness, goodness, faithfulness, gentleness, and self-control.'"

Lizzy understood about half of what he was saying about the spirit but thought that if every person would live by this fruit, there would be no more wars, hate, injustice, or prejudice, and that everyone would just love one another. "What a wonderful world that would be," she said to herself.

The young man got back up and sang the song "In Christ Alone." While he sang, Brad gave an invitation. "Anyone here who would like to meet Christ for themselves, come up to the front and surrender your heart. I promise you will never regret it."

At the end, Brad gave one last instruction. "Our next week's schedule will be posted on our webpage, or you can call the church for the taped recording. I really appreciate all of you coming tonight and everyone's prayers."

When everyone had left, Brad inquired, "So, what did you think, Lizzy?"

"I really liked it." She didn't want to tell him that it sounded like a foreign language to her. "I will probably be 'down' again next week." She added, "If you and your wife would like to come for a meal, I can make you something to eat at no charge."

Brad gave another heartfelt laugh. "I don't have a wife, Lizzy. Up until now I haven't had the time." He added, "Thanks again, and I may take you up on the meal since our kitchen flooded." Brad had been living in a studio apartment attached to the back of the church, which also flooded. He really was touched and taken aback by Lizzy's gracious offer.

"Sure. Anytime. Good night."

Brad said, "Good night," and walked out the door.

Lizzy locked up, turned out the lights, and went upstairs. Her head could barely absorb all the events of the day. She'd never thought when she woke up this morning the way the day would have turned out. She could not believe that Brad wasn't married. Thoughts of him ran through her mind like a movie in slow motion. She had really enjoyed the church service and wished she had tried it out much sooner. While she was lying in bed, she felt a funny, energized feeling that was new for her. It was many hours before her eyes finally shut for the night.

CHAPTER 3

Monday morning started like every other day for Lizzy. She rolled out of bed in her flannel pajamas, slipped on her fuzzy robe, and proceeded into the kitchen. She would always start the day with that first cup of coffee that had already been brewed, set by a timer, by her Mr. Coffee machine. She would say to herself she needed that coffee jump-start in the morning, or the day wasn't going to happen. Then she moved to her dining room table, which doubled as her office and was an organized clutter. She sat down facing the river to watch the sun cast its glow over the mountains. Today was not one of those sunny days, and there was no glow. In fact, Pittsburgh was just behind Seattle, Washington, as far as cloudy days went. With over two hundred cloudy days a year, Lizzy sometimes wondered if that was the reason why she was often fatigued. She took a big gulp of her coffee, then pulled the receipts and money out of the bag to get it ready for the bank deposit later. After she finished counting, she filled out the deposit slip along with the cash, put it into a blue bag and set it aside. She then took her credit card receipts, stacked them, opened her laptop, and turned it on.

Lizzy's dad used to have an accountant named Butch in Oakmont, but she could no longer could afford that luxury. She had to teach herself how to do accounting and taxes. She found QuickbooksPro for accounting and Turbo Tax for taxes. She always gave her fair share in quarterly state sales taxes and federal taxes for fear that she might get audited. She was a quick learner and smart about using the computer. Lizzy liked how adaptable she was, and this gave her confidence.

She had learned online banking and now reconciled her credit card deposits. She kept a close eye on her daily balance and borrowed from her own credit card only if needed, especially now in the winter months, when business was extremely slow. She knew things would pick up in the spring when she could open the deck out back. She had added rainbow umbrellas to the tables. People would come from Oakmont on their way downtown to eat and make her place a stop to have a drink or an appetizer and to enjoy the relaxing sound of the river and admire the surreal view. Money was always on her mind these days, but so far, she had managed to keep the Allegheny River Pub afloat.

Lizzy finished her paperwork, then showered and made breakfast, allowing time for her hair to air-dry. She always ate the same thing for breakfast, something her mom called "a toad in the hole." Lizzy had always laughed when Mom said that. She would jokingly reply, "Who wants to eat a toad?" Lizzy knew it wasn't a frog, but an egg in a round hole that had been cut into the center of a piece of bread and fried in a skillet with butter. She thought whoever had come up with the recipe was an inventive person, because you could have an egg and toast all at once, like a one-stop shop.

She washed down the "frog" with a glass of orange juice, put the dishes in the dishwasher, pulled back her hair, and headed downstairs. The stairs were inside the building facing the parking lot, and at the bottom was the entry to the pub. There also was another spiral staircase upstairs on the other side by the kitchen that Lizzy's dad had put in as a fire escape when Vickie was born. Lizzy turned left into the pub and flipped on the lights on the left wall. She then said, "Let the games begin," giving herself a pep talk.

Lizzy went through her mental checklist. She felt like if she could keep everything in order, the day would run smoothly. She took a #10 can of chicken noodle soup and poured it into a slow cooker then placed the cooker back into the refrigerator. She would start it at 2:00 so it was ready at 3:00, when she opened. The rest of the daily specials Lizzy would place on the prep stand. Today, she took out mashed potato flakes, a can of gravy, and a can of mixed vegetables. She put the appropriate-sized pans on the stove so they would be ready to use later. Lizzy had made two trays of meat loaf the day before. She would bake one of the trays at 2:00 and the other, if needed, at 5:00. After the tray was done cooking, she would refrigerate it and then take out a single serving, place it into the microwave along with mashed potatoes, gravy, and mixed vegetables, and serve it on the plate that way. That was definitely not the way Mom and Grandma would have done it; everything they made was from scratch. They were in the kitchen all day, starting in the earliest part of the morning. But Lizzy reminded herself that she was only one person, so her shortcut cooking methodology would have to suffice. Besides that, it was working just fine at the moment—at least that's what she convinced herself—but she asked herself often, *Is it as good? Absolutely not!*

Lizzy took an inventory of her supplies and the liquor she had on hand. If she was short, she made a list to be ordered or to pick up at the liquor store later. She then put the containers of used oil outside the garage door and took the trash to the dumpster. Someone in the neighborhood picked up the used oil for free because he used it in his car after he converted it to fuel. Lizzy sometimes imagined how bad that car must have smelt inside, and that outside it must have smelt like a French fry car going by. Not that it mattered to her; she was just glad she didn't have to deal with that smelly used grease, and it was an easy way to get rid of it.

Since it was Monday, she didn't have to do her morning cleaning because she had done it the day before. So, she flipped on the TV, sat down on a chair by the table closest to it, and watched the news while she drank a Sprite. On the big screen, much to Lizzy's surprise, was Brad Schmidt on KDKA News. He did not look at all nervous, she thought, perhaps because he talked in front of people all the time. He was wearing the same shirt he'd had on when he was unloading the pews, but in Lizzy's mind he looked even more handsome.

The reporter stated, "The initial fire marshal's report concluded the fire looked suspicious because the door was jammed open and there appeared to be some sort of accelerant, but the report won't be totally conclusive until the lab reports return." The reporter then looked at Brad and asked, "Do you have any idea why someone would do this?"

"I don't think this was an act of hate because nothing was broken." He continued, "Whoever it was broke into our petty cash box, kept in the front office. Perhaps they were trying to cover their trail with a fire. Regardless of who and why, it's going to take several months and a substantial amount of money to repair the water damage. Unfortunately, we are a small church with a limited amount of funds. This is definitely going to be a hardship and will set us back while we wait for the insurance company's investigation."

The reporter then asked Brad, "Is it true you are now holding your services at the Allegheny River Pub?"

"Yes, our kind neighbor Lizzy Murphy, owner of the pub, has graciously agreed to allow us to hold services there in her empty garage, until repairs are completed," he added. "We just moved our pews here today, and we are planning a service tonight."

The reporter concluded, "We will keep you informed when details of the investigation unfold. The local police are asking for help. If anyone has any information, they are to call the Verona Police Department. But for now, the First Baptist Church of Verona can be called the Pub Pews Church of Verona." The news reporter ended with, "Back to you in the studio."

Lizzy's mouth dropped open when the pub's phone rang. She was still in disbelief that the pub had been mentioned, and that she herself was mentioned by name in a good way. She walked over to the phone and answered. "Hello, Allegheny River Pub, this is Lizzy speaking." On the line was Suzie Quaid, her bartender, who wasn't scheduled to come in until the next day because Lizzy always worked on Mondays.

Suzie Quaid, aka Suzie Q, had been an employee of the pub well before Lizzy acquired it from her dad. Suzie was a petite, energetic person, but she was strong as nails. Suzie Q could run circles around Lizzy keeping every glass filled, and she could also double as a cook and a waitress. She and Lizzy had become very close friends over the last twelve years, and Lizzy called her "her right-hand woman." Lizzy would be lost without her.

"Lizzy, this is Suzie Q. Did you see the news yet?"

"Yes, I just now saw it."

"What did I miss over the weekend? What did you think about the story?" And without missing a beat Suzie Q added, "But most importantly, how was the hottie preacher man?"

Lizzy chuckled. "First of all, I was surprised as you about the church fire because I didn't hear a thing until the 'preacher man,' Brad, came knocking at the door Sunday morning." She continued, "As far as the story goes, I am glad that it was so positive." Lizzy sighed. "Brad is not only hot, but he's also kind, considerate, and most importantly, single." Lizzy laughed. She wouldn't have said that to anyone else but Suzie Q. Lizzy added, "The church is paying me to rent the space to them, but after seeing the news this morning, I feel guilty about taking any money. I may just let them use the space for free."

"Don't you dare not take the money, Lizzy! You need it as much or more than they do. You are too generous, and that is part of your problem."

Lizzy admitted she had her dad's soft heart, but somehow, as much as she needed the money, she didn't think she would keep it. Money wasn't going to make or break her. It was more important to help a neighbor in need, and she decided she was going to return Brad's check.

Lizzy and Suzie Q spent fifteen more minutes on the phone going over the details about Sunday, when finally Lizzy said, "I better get going, Suzie. I will fill in the blanks tomorrow when you come to work. See you then. Bye."

Lizzy had just hung up the phone when another call came in. She picked up the phone and said, "Hello, Allegheny River Pub. This is Lizzy speaking." She could hear the voice on the other line say, "Hi, Lizzy, this is Carlos."

Carlos Jorge was her other permanent full-time worker whom she had hired about five years before. Carlos, nicknamed CJ, worked at a gym in Oakmont as a personal trainer during the day and at the pub at night until closing. He worked six days a week except for holidays or when he needed to take a vacation to take his wife and kids to visit her family. He had started to work at the pub when he responded to the ad that

Lizzy posted on Craigslist for a bouncer. At the time, Lizzy had had a few incidents where someone came in and had a few too many drinks. She called them the "Jekyll and Hyde" drinkers. Most people who drank got happy. Not the "Jekyll and Hyde" type—they got nasty and liked to fight. That was when she decided to close the pub at midnight instead of 2 a.m. and find a bouncer for protection.

During the interview, Lizzy told Carlos he might have to fill in as a busboy and a dishwasher, which he gladly agreed to do. Lizzy was delighted that CJ had said yes. He was built like an armored truck, very muscular and tall. He was a true lifesaver because of his willingness to help wherever he was needed, and his presence had stopped any more of those silly incidents. CJ and Suzie Q had become her only family now.

Carlos, like Suzie, asked many questions about what had happened on Sunday. He, too, had seen the interview on the TV at the gym. He laughed and told Lizzy that he and his family might have to miss Mass and come to the pub instead. The whole thought of going to work to go to church amused him. He told her through his laughter he would see her later at the "pub pews" church. CJ was still snickering when she finally hung up the phone.

Lizzy turned out the lights, threw on her wool coat, then took her blue bag, purse, and car keys out the door to go to the bank. The bank was going to be it for today as far as errands went. She was still reeling about the interview as she drove out of the parking lot. The car might have been moving slowly, but her mind was traveling a million miles an hour.

CHAPTER 4

Lizzie ate a sandwich and some potato chips, then put her feet up for a while before going downstairs to the pub at two o'clock to start the soup and to get the bar ready with sliced lemons, limes, and ice. She would get the cashbox out of the safe located in her closet behind her shoes. She put the check she received from Brad in the cash register till and headed down the stairs after she locked her door to the apartment.

In the pub, she turned on the lights and the TV and plugged in the billiard lights. Lizzy found that her regular customers preferred the TV on when they came in from work. The TV would usually go off around nine o'clock and the jukebox came on until midnight.

A regular group of people came in almost every night. Lizzy called them the "patrons." The first one to come in would be Bonnie Spencer, around three o'clock. She was the owner of the beauty salon called A Hair Above. Bonnie had originally lived and worked in a salon in Oakmont. She'd moved to Verona in 2006 when her son, Tony, was born. There were rumors that Tony was the son of married Joe Russo, the owner of the auto repair shop on the main street of town. Joe had provided the financing for Bonnie's salon. Lizzy didn't put much merit in the rumor because she really liked Bonnie. She admired Bonnie for raising her two sons on her own. Tony was thirteen years old, and her youngest son, Ian, was eight. She thought Bonnie worked hard and had solid business sense, which was the common thread between the two. Besides that, Bonnie always trimmed Lizzy's hair for free. But mostly Lizzy loved Bonnie's transparent honesty and her genuinely good heart. Lizzy thought of her as a surrogate sister.

Bonnie had once been a beautiful woman with her own original shade of blond hair. She had a flawless creamy complexion that now was showing some signs of stress. Her son Tony was becoming rebellious. He had become disrespectful, unruly, and truant. Bonnie was worried that he was setting a bad example for his younger brother, Ian. He seemed to be heading down the wrong path. He had started hanging out with two fifteen-year-old boys. Their names were Pete and Kyle, and they were also being raised by single moms. There was a rumor they were all trying to organize a gang called the River Rats. Nevertheless, Bonnie felt helpless and she wasn't sure how to fix the problem. Lizzy would try to console her friend, but not having any kids as a reference point, she could do little but listen to her.

The next patrons to come in at five o'clock were the Summer Funeral Home brothers. They were the third-generation owners of the successful funeral home located on Colorado Street in Verona. The funeral home itself was a large, stately Victorian house. They had a good reputation and would draw a lot of business from Oakmont. Ken was the oldest brother. He was a tall gray-haired man, very serious; he never cracked a smile. Lizzy thought maybe some of his work was wearing off on him. He usually met his wife, Irene, at the pub. They would always eat the blue plate special, then order a beer and a Crown Royal. Lizzy thought they didn't seem all that happy or unhappy with life; with very few words spoken between them, they would always eat and run.

Right on the heels of Ken, his brother, Teddy, would come into the pub. Lizzy thought there couldn't be more opposite brothers than those two. Teddy was extroverted, social, talkative, and always smiling. He would talk to anyone who would talk back with him. However, he would mostly drink his dinner with beer. When he ate, he ordered some wings with fries, which accounted for his rather large belly. He was divorced with an autistic grown son who was institutionalized. Lizzy felt the two brothers had no love for each other because they would treat each other like total strangers. Teddy seemed to be drowning his loneliness; perhaps he felt like a failure as a father. Or maybe he drank in excess to drown out the death he encountered every day in his occupation. Either way, Lizzy wished he could find some happiness outside of a beer mug.

At six o'clock, other different groups came into the pub. The first were Bonnie's employees from the salon, Crystal Stall and Maggie Jones. They were both in their early twenties and could be considered pretty. Lizzy liked them both but thought they were always selling themselves short. They were always in search of the perfect man, but they gave too much of themselves away right away to attract a really decent man.

The second group to come in were the young men from the Daily Juice Factory. The factory was located by the bridge on Allegheny River Boulevard. It was the largest employer in town, employing over eight hundred people. It produced cocktail mixes and little jugs of juice called "Hugs."

Lizzy called the Daily young men the "three amigos." Their names were Bill Wells, Bob Gooding, and Brian Smart. They were all fairly good-looking young men in their twenties. Bill was tall, with brown eyes and hair. Bob was shorter, with blond hair and blue eyes. And Brian was medium height with brown hair and eyes. They shared a house a few blocks away in town. They always ordered the blue plate specials, telling Lizzy that she cooked better than their moms. They would drink a couple of pitchers of draft beer at night. They threw darts, played pool, and were the ones who always initiated the jukebox. They stayed until closing and always left happily together. Lizzy thought they were nice young men, even though she felt like they lacked direction because their conversations were always the same day after day, and their lives rotated around hanging out at the pub every night. When asked why they weren't dating, the reply always was that "women are too expensive."

David Smith, a disabled Afghanistan war veteran, came in next. He had a prosthetic leg and walked with a cane. He had lost his leg when his fellow soldier and friend stepped on an improvised explosive device (IED). Losing his leg was a much better outcome than his friend experience; the friend lost his life. Lizzy thought David might be suffering from depression or PTSD (post-traumatic stress disorder). He always sat at the far end of the bar playing the trivia game that sat on top of the bar. He was a handsome man with sandy blond hair and brown eyes. While he was sitting at the bar, no one would suspect that he was missing a leg. He kept to himself, and if Lizzy could get him to say a word, it was a miracle. She thought he was no trouble, but she wished she could climb into his darkness and pull him into the light, where he might find some happiness. She couldn't imagine what he had experienced and what he must have seen, but she never broached the subject with him and he never, ever brought it up.

Finally, Joe Russo, the owner of Auto Plus, would come in the pub and stay for one or two drinks. He was a good-looking Italian man with dark hair and dark, piercing eyes. He would sit next to Bonnie at the bar. Bonnie and Joe always had a low-toned conversation about what, nobody knew except them. He always paid for Bonnie's food and drink and left a large tip. He would leave no later than seven o'clock in the evening to get home to his wife and kids.

Occasionally other people came into the pub. Lizzy called them the "street people" because they walked in and out after a drink, never to be seen again. She called the crowd when she opened the outside deck the "summer people." Lizzy had developed good relationships with her regular summer people, and over the years they had never failed to return. She knew their names and stories and made sure they knew she appreciated their business. She always put a little extra TLC into their food and service.

CHAPTER 5

Lizzy finally had everything ready to open the pub. The meat loaf, mashed potatoes, gravy, and vegetables were done, and the chicken noodle soup was hot. She also turned on the fryer to heat the oil. The cash box was ready, and the bar had everything needed to start the day. The lights and TV were on, so at three o'clock Lizzy unlocked the doors. Several minutes passed before Bonnie, as predicted, walked through the doors.

"Hi." She couldn't help noticing that Bonnie looked like she hadn't slept for days. "You look terrible. What happened to you?"

Bonnie sat down on her usual stool and said, "It's Tony. He and his friend were out late Saturday night, and I was worried sick that something terrible had happened to him. I'm at the end of my rope. I don't think I can take much more." Bonnie began to sob.

Lizzy felt sad for her friend. She couldn't imagine how disheartened Bonnie must feel. Lizzy didn't know what to say at this point. "I am sorry, Bonnie. I wish I could do something to help. Are there any agencies that might provide help?"

Bonnie shook her head, then grabbed a Kleenex from her purse and blew her nose. "He needs a man's hand to knock some sense into him. A man who can relate to the changes Tony is going through. He is like a little boy trapped in a grown man's body. Some days I don't think he likes himself either."

Lizzy asked Bonnie if she wanted something to eat or drink. Bonnie nodded her head. She brought out a plate of food for Bonnie just as Brad Schmidt walked in and sat down a few stools away from Bonnie. Lizzy introduced Brad to Bonnie and explained to her about the fire at the church. Bonnie was surprised but said that she hadn't watched the news because she had been having trouble with her teenage son.

Lizzy had a thought. "Brad, you mentioned you were a youth minister. Do you think you could talk to Tony?"

"Yes, I would be happy to." He handed Bonnie a business card with his phone number and told her she could call anytime. She could let him know what time would work for her, when Tony was home, and where she lived. Bonnie felt relieved, as she would take any help she could get.

Brad looked at Lizzy. "Do you have a minute?" he asked. When she said yes, they moved over to one of the tables by the glass sliding doors.

"First, I hope you were okay with me sharing your place and name on the news. Second, I was wondering if we could move the church service to eleven o'clock this coming Sunday? And lastly, could the church pay you to prepare a spaghetti buffet lunch after our service?"

Lizzy liked that Brad was to the point and direct with his questions. "Yes, I was fine with you using my name and the pub's name on the news. I thought that was nice of you. Yes, you can move the service to eleven o'clock. And finally, yes, I can do the buffet if you are willing to shop with me and helping with the preparation and cleanup."

Brad agreed to all the conditions. Lizzy and Brad finalized the arrangements and decided to meet and shop on Friday at eleven o'clock at the "Strip District" in downtown Pittsburgh on Penn Avenue. Lizzy shopped there every Friday morning as part of her weekly routine. The Strip District was a destination spot of several blocks that contained restaurants, specialty food stores, gift stores, and street vendors. Lizzy specifically went to Wholey's Fish Market to purchase the fish for Friday's night fish fry at the pub.

Brad seemed relieved. "Now, with that done, can I order one of your blue plate specials? I saw the meat loaf yesterday, and it looked great. Besides that, it's one of my favorite meals."

"No problem, and let me guess—you want a Sprite to drink?"

Brad chuckled. "You got it." He really liked the easy-going and playful mannerisms Lizzy possessed. He already felt a friendship growing with her.

Lizzy served up his plate with bigger portions than normal and delivered the plate and the drink to his table. She also brought with her the check that Brad had given her the day before for renting the garage.

Brad thanked Lizzy and made a comment about how beautiful and peaceful the view was, even during the winter. "This meat loaf looks as good as what my mom used to make."

Lizzy handed Brad the check he had given her to rent the garage.

"What is this?"

Lizzy explained that she didn't think it was right to keep the check. She felt like the church could use it more.

Brad was taken aback by the kind act that Lizzy had just displayed. "I wasn't going to tell you, but I prayed all last night about our finances, and the most awesome thing happened this morning. Michael and Cindy Landry from Casey's restaurant called—you know, the trendy breakfast and lunch spot in Oakmont. They saw the story and pledged twenty-five thousand dollars as a donation to use as I see fit. That is why I thought of a spaghetti dinner. I invited the Landrys to church on Sunday, and they agreed, so the congregation can personally thank them then.

"It was very kind of you to return the check, but I insist you keep it. I will pay for the supplies for the banquet dinner on Sunday and give you two hundred dollars for your time, as well." With that, he took a bite of his meat loaf. "I insist I pay for this delicious meat loaf, too. If my mom were alive today, I am sure she would agree that this meat loaf is better than hers."

After Brad had eaten, paid his bill, and walked out, Lizzy thought that if a prayer could do all of that for Brad, maybe she should start praying too. Lizzy had to put those thoughts into practice and pray to get through the night when not only did all of her usual patrons show up, but there were ten new faces who came in as well. They said they had heard the news story on TV and hadn't realized that there was an eating spot by the river. After their meals, they raved about the cooking and promised to be back and bring friends with them next time.

By midnight, Lizzy was exhausted in a good way. She had sold every plate of food and then some. The cashbox was full, and to her recollection she hadn't been that busy for a long time. If it hadn't been for CJ's help, Lizzy was sure she would have sunk. She handed him an extra forty dollars and told him thanks and to go home. She would finish up cleaning the pub.

After letting CJ out, Lizzy sat down at the bar with a Sprite and reflected on how her luck had changed the minute she'd met Brad. She felt something for him that she had never experienced before. She thought maybe it wasn't really just luck. She should put more effort into this God whom Brad prayed to, and maybe this was her time to put her heart out there, too. It had been so long she'd been under lock and key, she wasn't sure if she remembered how.

CHAPTER 6

Beware of what you wish for, Lizzy thought to herself, when the pub was slammed with business all week. Some of the new people not only said they would be back for more food, but they said they'd be back for church on Sunday. Lizzy didn't realize that a news story would have that kind of positive impact on her business.

Now it was already Friday. She had been looking forward to a break from the pub, but mostly, she was looking forward to seeing Brad and showing him around the Strip District. The day was brisk but sunny, which she found lucky for the month of March. She hadn't seen him since Monday, figuring he was busy cleaning up the mess at the church. She thought maybe she would go down there and offer him some assistance, but she had been so busy herself. She did, however, think about him most of the week. In her mind, she would see his face—and his smile. There was a presence of peace around him. She really wasn't sure what to call it, but somehow, he was making his way into her heart. She was attracted to that sense of peace; in her line of work, she rarely had seen it.

Right at eleven o'clock, Brad showed up at the door of the pub and knocked. Lizzy came out wearing her ski parka and scarf and with her purse draped over her shoulder. She gave him a big smile back. "Are you ready for some fun?"

"I sure am. I have always wanted to go to the Strip. I've heard people talk about it, and now I get to go with a true professional," Brad said with a smile. Brad was having some strong feelings toward Lizzy, but voices in his mind, from the past, kept reminding him that he should be evenly spiritually yoked with his future spouse, so he was beating down his attraction for her as best as he could.

Lizzy giggled. "I grew up going to the Strip District. Some kids went to Kennywood Amusement Park. I went to the Strip instead. I guess you could say it was my roller coaster."

Brad smiled and got into the passenger side of Lizzy's car. Lizzy got behind the steering wheel, and they headed down River Boulevard, following the river toward downtown Pittsburgh. The conversation was filled with light pleasantries and a run-down of what they had done that week. They both agreed there had been less stressful and smoother weeks than the past one. When they arrived at the Strip, Lizzy pulled into a "Reserved" spot in front of Primanti Brothers restaurant on Eighteenth Street.

Brad questioned Lizzy. "How does this work that you get a reserved spot?"

"Like I said, my family has come here for years and developed friendships with a lot of the people here. I always hear what a great-grandpa and father I had." Lizzy then continued, "In other words, it's not what you know but who you know." Lizzy got out of the car and said, "This is our first stop. I am going to treat you to one of my favorite sandwiches."

Brad was flattered that Lizzy wanted to pay for his lunch, but he was more impressed that she wanted to share one of her favorite things with him. "This is your turf. You are in charge." They walked to a table in the back that was also marked "Reserved." He smiled at her. "Of course, you must 'know' some people." They both broke out in laughter.

Lizzy took charge and ordered two of Primanti's famous Pitts-burger sandwiches and two Sprites. Lizzy pulled out her list and showed Brad. "I hope you don't mind that I mapped out our day. I thought I would expedite our schedule, since I need to be back by three o'clock to open the pub."

Brad replied, "That's actually very nice of you. I am so happy that you are doing this for me. I can tell that you are a very kind and caring person. I really appreciate you helping me, and I appreciate you, too."

Lizzy was sure that her face had turned a bright shade of red. "Thanks," she said, just as the food arrived. The server set in front of them two large plates, each with a monstrosity of a sandwich, filled with shaved grilled meat, melted cheese, an oil and vinegar–based coleslaw, French fries, and tomato slices, stacked between two thick slices of Italian bread.

Brad's eyes became like saucers. "Wow, that is quite a sandwich. It's new to me to have the side dishes on the sandwich itself. I can't wait to try it, but I'm not sure if I can get my mouth around it."

Lizzy giggled. "That's what I said when I ate my first Pitts-burger, but believe me, you will figure it out pretty fast." Brad liked Lizzy's quick, humorous responses and her ability to make light of situations. He felt like she was the most upbeat person he'd met, although part of him wondered how much of it was put on. He felt a sense of discontent in her at times, but he couldn't be sure. She was like a puzzle with one piece missing in the middle.

Lizzy discussed the menu for the buffet with Brad while they ate. They agreed to serve three different pasta dishes in large chafing dishes on warmers, along with salad and Italian bread. Lizzy explained to Brad the three pastas 'they were going to make'—just as a reminder that he had agreed to help in the preparation. They were spaghetti with a red meat sauce, a red sauce with no meat over rigatoni, and chicken carbonara over rigatoni. She explained that she had hosted Italian nights at the pub over the years, and they were very successful. Brad thought it sounded great to him and trusted Lizzy's expertise. Lizzy enjoyed making buffet food, and she told Brad about her dream to take the garage and convert it into a wedding reception hall. This was the first indication Brad caught that Lizzy really didn't want to be a pub owner after all; she wanted to change the pub into something else. There seemed to be something missing in her story that she hadn't told him yet, and he really wanted to find out what it was.

They had just finished their sandwiches when the manager came by to greet Lizzy. They talked for a few minutes, then Lizzy paid the bill and they walked out into the street and turned right toward Penn Avenue.

Brad felt like he had crossed the ocean and landed in a European street market. There were street vendors selling souvenir shirts and hats supporting the Pittsburgh Steelers, the Pittsburgh Penguins, and the University of Pittsburgh. Vendors were cooking all sorts of ethnic foods on the sidewalk, creating a potpourri of delicious aromas. Flower vendors and candy vendors seemed to be on every corner. Brad was amazed. The Strip District was much more than he'd expected, and the hustle-bustle atmosphere was new to him—and contagious.

"What's our first stop?" he asked Lizzy.

She turned to him to answer. "We are going to the Macaroni Company for most of our dinner ingredients. We need olive oil, two containers of spaghetti sauce and one of carbonara sauce, onions, garlic, shredded mozzarella cheese, Parmesan cheese, salad greens, tomatoes, olives, Italian dressing, garlic bread, and spaghetti and rigatoni noodles. Then we'll take everything back to the car before we go to our next stop, Parma Meats.

"But the real first stop is right here at Mon Aimee Chocolate for one of their truffles. It always makes shopping more enjoyable." Lizzy gave Brad a big smile, and he realized how endearing she was. He still couldn't believe she had lived just down the street the whole time without him knowing it. He definitely wanted to know more about her.

They went through the Macaroni Company with their list and collected all the needed ingredients. Lizzy seemed to know the Italian wholesale store like the back of her hand, and much to his surprise, shopping with her was fun. Ordinarily, Brad didn't like to shop—ever. At the checkout, Brad paid with the church's charge card, and they took the multiple bags back to the car.

Brad turned to Lizzy. "One down. Now off to Parma Meats. Is that all?"

"No, I also have to go to Wholey's Fish Market to pick up thirty pounds of cod for my fish fry tonight. But that's just at the pickup window. They'll add it to my account and I pay once a month. So, that errand is an in and out."

"Great. What kind of meat are we getting at Parma?"

"We need two pounds of ground meat, two pounds of Italian sausage, four pounds of chicken breast, and one pound of prosciutto," Lizzy read off the list.

They had started down the street to Parma Meats when Brad abruptly stopped in front of a flower stand and pointed to a big bouquet of yellow roses. He handed the man a ten-dollar bill, picked up the bouquet, and walked over to Lizzy. "Here's to your help and friendship."

Lizzy was caught off guard with the gesture, not only because of the flowers, but because he had upgraded their working relationship into a 'friendship.' She not only felt honored, but she had some sort of strange feeling in her stomach—she wondered if it was "butterflies," but she graciously accepted them.

Brad and Lizzy arrived at Parma Meats and walked in. The store was crowded, and someone at the door was handing out numbers as people entered. Brad had never seen so many different kinds of meats. At least ten employees were working behind the glass display case with white aprons; some had red blood stains on their aprons, and everyone wore gloves. Lizzy and Brad stepped out of the way toward the front of the store to wait for their number to be called, which was going to be awhile.

Lizzy turned to Brad. "So, what do you think so far?"

"I forgot I was still in Pittsburgh. I feel like I am in a different country." Then he added, "I am truly amazed, but I am really enjoying myself. I would like to come back again."

"Well, now that you know your way around, you certainly can do that."

"No, I meant I would like to come back with you." He smiled and gazed deeply into Lizzy's eyes.

Lizzy took an awkward pause and looked back into Brad's blue eyes. "I would like that."

Parma Meats finally called their number. They collected the bags full of meat and headed across the street to Wholey's Fish Market. Brad once again couldn't believe the number of different fish the market had lining the forty-foot wall. Most of them were whole fish resting on top of ice. Brad wondered how many fish eyes there were, when Lizzy gave his arm a tug and led him to the pickup window. She gave the person at the window her name and account number. The man handed her a box, but Brad intervened, grabbing the box instead, and said, "Allow me to carry that." Lizzy nodded her head with a smile.

Lizzy looked at her watch and said, "We are right on schedule. We can head back now. Suzie Q is coming today, and we will prepare the sauces today. We can prepare the rest of the dinner and set up the tables early on Sunday morning. I will prepare the salad tomorrow and put it into the refrigerator. That will save us a lot of stress trying to prepare everything the same day."

"Sounds like a good plan," he said as he positioned himself into the car.

When they got back to the pub, they took the box and the many bags of ingredients into the kitchen.

Brad said with a smile, "What do you want me to do now, boss?"

Lizzy laughed. "We need to make room on the counters, so let's put things away first. All the cold items, such as the salad, tomatoes, onions, garlic, and meats, go into the walk-in refrigerator. The rest can go on the shelves. I will leave some cod out tonight to thaw in the refrigerator, too.

"Your job will be to cut the onions and garlic to add to the sauces. I used to make the sauces from scratch, but I've found the premade sauces with added onions, garlic, and spices were just about as good. I am pretty sure Grandma and Mom would not approve, and they are probably rolling in their graves right now," she said with a chuckle.

"Grab an apron, one of those cutting boards, a sharp knife, and a bag of onions and garlic. Place them on the prep station and wash your hands. Most foodborne illnesses come from unwashed hands."

"I didn't know that. I guess I am learning all sorts of new things today." He chuckled.

Lizzy softly laughed. "I learned a lot about food safety when I took the food certification class from the Allegheny County Health Board. I was amazed how many different ways people can get sick from food. It almost made me not want to serve it. I work really hard not to cross-contaminate the food I serve. I would never want anyone to get sick.

"When you are done with that job, grab a new clean cutting board and knife, and cube the chicken breast. Put the chicken pieces into that steel bowl. All the dirty dishes and knives go into that blue sanitizing water in the right-hand sink. I will wash everything when we are done."

"I know. Then I will wash my hands again."

Lizzy smiled. "You really are a quick study." They both laughed out loud.

Lizzy placed two big stock pots on the stove and poured oil on the bottoms of them. She opened the canned sauces and placed them nearby. Brad diced the onions and garlic, then cubed the chicken. She started the gas stove and put approximately four cups of onions and a half cup of garlic in one of the pots. Into the other pot she put two cups of onions and a quarter cup of garlic. She sautéed the onions and garlic in both pots until they caramelized. She then added the ground beef and sausage to brown in one pot, and she added the cubed chicken to the other pot until fully cooked. She had already placed colanders in steel pans to drain off the excess fat.

Lizzy asked Brad, "If you don't mind, can you drain each of these pots into the colanders, then place the contents back into the pots?"

"Sure, I would be glad to."

Lizzy grabbed the glass container of her homemade spice blends, which contained oregano, basil, thyme, rosemary, and sage. She then pulled out a jar of cinnamon and put a pinch into each of the pots. She told Brad, "You can stir this pot, and I will stir the others. We will let them simmer then cool before we put them into the walk-in refrigerator for Sunday morning to marry them with the pastas."

While they were stirring, their conversation came back to the wedding reception hall. Brad thought Lizzy would be great at that after seeing her magic in the kitchen.

"I couldn't help but notice you added cinnamon."

Lizzy giggled. "Yes, that is something my grandma JoJo taught me. She said it was her secret to enhancing the flavors—she referred to it as a 'tongue stimulator.' Now that you know that, you must never tell anyone else."

Brad grinned. "I promise I won't tell."

Then, out of the blue, Brad asked, "Do you have a boyfriend?"

"No! I haven't got the time for that. I spent all my time here, and besides, the guys who come in here I would never consider boyfriend material."

Brad nodded and thought Lizzy would make a great girlfriend. Deep in his mind, she reminded him of his mom. He loved his mom's personality and qualities. He thought with a chuckle, "Maybe men do like someone like their moms."

Right after they had put the stock pots into the refrigerator and cleaned up the kitchen, Suzie Q appeared after letting herself in.

"Wow, there's a good-looking man in the kitchen. That is something I don't see every day." Suzie Q laughed.

"Oh, Suzie Q, it is no wonder why you get so many big tips. This is Brad Schmidt, the pastor I told you about. We went to the Strip today to get ingredients for his buffet and made the sauces for Sunday. So, don't be sneaking a bite of those sauces. Do you hear me?" Lizzy said in a very bubbly voice.

"It's nice to meet you, Brad. I have heard a lot about you. Who knows? If I can get my kids and husband out of bed on Sunday, maybe we will come check out your sermon."

"It is nice to meet you, Suzie. I have heard a lot about you, too. The service is at eleven o'clock, so maybe you can get your crew up for that. Besides that, we are having an Italian buffet afterward. There, you won't have to sneak."

Suzie giggled and said to Lizzy, "I like him already." She then winked and gave their signal for "hot" to Lizzy when Brad turned his back.

"So, what time would you like me to be back on Sunday?" Brad asked

"I think around nine o'clock would give us enough time to get everything prepared and set up. Do you want to stay for some fish and chips now? I made the fish batter earlier, and it comes with fries. It is the least I can do for your help carrying the heavy box of fish."

"That sounds really good, but only if you will join me," Brad said with a grin.

Suzie Q piped in, "Lizzy would be happy to do that, and I am happy to prepare the food for you two."

"I feel like I have been ambushed." Lizzy smiled. "Let me go upstairs and get the cashbox for the register, and then you two win."

Brad and Lizzy enjoyed the fish, but more so, they enjoyed the conversation. They talked about politics and a variety of other topics. They discovered that they shared conservative philosophies as well as common interests like hiking, biking, movies, and bowling.

Finally, Brad told Lizzy that he had had a wonderful time but he needed to start his sermon for Sunday. In his mind he wanted it to be an extra-special sermon in case the Landrys came from Casey's, but really he wanted to impress Lizzy. Lizzy walked him to the door just as David, the vet, was walking in.

David said, "Hey, you're the guy whose church had a fire. I am really sorry about that. If you need any help, tell Lizzy, and she can get ahold of me."

Lizzy's mouth no doubt dropped open, because that was the most speech she had ever heard coming out of David's mouth at one time. She thought again that Brad had a presence about him. If he could get David to talk, that was the proof in the pudding.

Brad waved to Lizzy. "I will see you Sunday at nine."

"Thanks. See you then." She waved back.

David sat down at his usual spot in front of the trivia game and ordered his usual beer. He asked Suzie Q about Sunday. When she finished giving him the schedule, he said, "I think I might check out the church. You know how I like Lizzy's Italian cooking."

Suzie Q thought to herself that if David was thinking about going to church, she wanted to see that. She knew she was the boss of her house, and her husband, and now her two kids didn't have a fighting chance to stay in bed on Sunday. Church, unbeknownst to them, was in their future.

CHAPTER 7

Lizzy thought Friday was dreamy and fun. It was quite a contrast to Friday night, which was a borderline nightmare. Thank goodness CJ was there to pick up the slack. She was in the kitchen all night. In hindsight she should have thawed the whole box of fish. She literally had to manually thaw the fish by running them under cool water. She had to pat them with paper towels until they were completely dry before she could batter and then fry them. She must have used three rolls of paper towels. She wouldn't be caught off guard again, but she decided she wasn't going to complain too much, either, because it was the first time ever that she'd sold out of her fish. People who tried the fish raved about the batter and loved that they could order it with one of the four different sauces or with wine vinegar. The four sauces were the same she used to coat the wings and were her secret recipes; there were hot, medium, or mild hot sauces, and a buttery garlic sauce. She thought people liked to spice up the fish by dipping. She used to make a tartar sauce but nobody ever asked for that, so she eliminated it from the menu. Regardless she was glad that the people enjoyed the fish.

Saturday, Lizzy prepared the salads, then cut up bread and placed them in baskets and put them into the refrigerator. She got two extra-large coolers that had wheels so when full they would be easy to roll; she filled one with water and one with sodas. She found checkered tablecloths and plastic flower centerpieces for the tables and brought down four card tables and chairs she had stored upstairs. She made a list of things to do for Sunday's buffet. She wanted it to be perfect for Brad.

The rest of the day was mostly uneventful. After cleaning, she put vegetable beef soup and put it into the warmer and prepared "hamburgers in paradise" for the daily special. She placed an order with Sysco for Monday. Her food supply was dwindling, and she told herself she was Old Mother Hubbard. She was sure the revenue numbers had jumped up considerably, so again she felt thankful. She also placed a beer and liquor order for delivery on Monday. Mostly, she thought about Brad coming tomorrow and had to snap herself out of thoughts of him throughout the day, telling herself, "Come on, Lizzy, concentrate."

Brad showed up Sunday exactly at nine with a bag in hand. He was dressed in casual attire. Lizzy couldn't help but notice how nice he looked and smelled as she unlocked the pub's door and let him in.

She asked curiously, "What do you have in the bag?"

"I have an old paint shirt to put over my clothes while we are working this morning to protect my clothes. I've also got my Bible, and here, I got you a Bible too, so you can't say I never gave you anything." Brad was making light of this, but deep down in his heart he wanted more than anything for Lizzy come to know the Lord.

Lizzy was so touched that she fought back tears. She looked at the leather book that had Bible in gold lettering on the front. In the lower right corner was inscribed her name, Lizzy Murphy. She said with a heartfelt tone, "Thank you, that was so very nice of you. I have always been curious about the book, and now I have my very own copy. I really appreciate it—and you too."

Brad and Lizzy went into the pub to start cooking and setting up for the banquet. Brad asked Lizzy what she wanted him to do first. She instructed him to get the banquet tables from the garage and place them by the windows. She wanted him to get from the shelves by the kitchen door, three of the four commercial warmers, but first she told him that inside of the warmers were three checkered tablecloths. She instructed him to spread those over the banquet tables, then place the warmers on top. After that, she had him grab all the sturdy paper plates, napkins, and plastic utensils and place them at the other end of the table.

"When you are done with that, report back here for your next assignment."

He smiled and saluted. "Yes, ma'am. Aye, aye, captain." He turned and proceeded to do as commanded. He really liked how Lizzy could make fun out of working and her playful manner of doing things.

Lizzy had already arranged the tables after she closed Saturday night by moving them closer to the bar. She added several card tables and chairs and covered all the tables with plastic tablecloths and silk flower arrangements she had purchased from the Dollar Store for occasions like this. She put the beautiful yellow roses that Brad had given her Friday behind the bar by the cash register.

Next Lizzy got busy in the kitchen. She warmed the premade sauces from Saturday and a spiced-up plain sauce on the back burners, while she boiled the noodles in two large stock pots on the front burners. Her intention was to combine the noodles and sauces, cover the chicken with the prosciutto, then top them (except the vegetarian pasta) with shredded mozzarella cheese. She would then cover them and place them in the oven on a low temperature. Right before the buffet she would place them into the warmers. She had prepared the day before one bowl of tomato and olive salad, and in another she had added some prosciutto, which she would toss in the Italian dressing right before the meal. She had several covered large baskets of sliced bread and butter pads that she would have Brad take to the tables next. Lizzy would never leave the kitchen with the stoves on, so she was glad Brad was helping her out.

Brad reported back to duty and asked Lizzy, "Is there anything else to be done?"

"Yes, there are two large coolers that I filled last night. One contains sodas and the other bottled waters. I need you to cover them with ice and take them along with the plastic cups to the end of the bar."

When Lizzy felt confident enough that all the ducks were in a row, she looked at Brad. "It's ten thirty, and it looks like we are ready. Do you want me to unlock the door now?"

"Yes, but let me take off my shirt and comb my hair first. Where is the bathroom?"

She looked at him in his very colorful splattered-paint shirt with his disheveled blond hair and said, "Through those doors on the right." She thought to herself, "That's another thing we have in common...he is a messy painter like I am a messy cook."

When Brad turned to head toward the bathroom, she asked, "Would you like a Sprite?" He nodded.

Brad came out of the bathroom looking good, with his hair stylishly slicked back and his blue button-down shirt and khaki pants clean and sharp. "Why don't we take our sodas into the garage in case someone decides to come early?"

Lizzy nodded, and they proceeded into the garage. Lizzy flipped on the lights and unlocked the entry door. She couldn't get over how nice the pews looked. They were still pristine and added character to the uneventful garage.

She informed Brad, "I hope you don't mind, but I am going to sit in the back pew today. I don't want you to be offended, but I want to leave a little earlier to put the food out."

Brad turned to her. "That is fine. I understand. Besides, I couldn't imagine you doing anything that would ever offend me." Just then, some members of the congregation came in, and Brad quickly went over to greet them.

Lizzy sat in the back and watched the steady stream of people arrive. She couldn't help but notice one couple who stood out, looking like they had just stepped out of a "Who's Who" publication. Lizzy counted fifty people total before the service started. She was relieved that there would be a sufficient amount of food. When Bonnie, David, and Suzie Q and her family walked in last, she gave them a big wave from the back row.

Before Brad started his sermon, a group of five young people went to the front. One had a guitar and sang a beautiful rendition of "Amazing Grace." Lizzy was truly moved by the words, and she found her eyes tearing up.

Brad talked about the Samaritan woman at the well, a story told in John 4:4–26 in the Bible. Most people opened their Bibles to the passage. Lizzy had thought to keep the Bible that Brad had given her earlier in a safe place upstairs, but she'd thought wrong. She felt a little embarrassed but probably only to herself. She noticed what a great storyteller Brad was and how he brought the passage to life. She had never heard about the "living water" that Jesus offered. She was intrigued, because Jesus said it was for an eternity and it could be hers too. She started to think of the simplicity of the story; it had an impact of hope, that no matter where you were in life (like stuck in a pub), it was just a small part in comparison to an eternity. She felt hope spring up inside of her, but then she noticed the time and silently got up and went into the kitchen, closing the door behind her, so as not to disturb Brad.

Lizzy finished up the last-minute preparations for the Italian buffet. The pastas, salads, and bread were all out. She placed bowls with grated Parmesan with spoons along with some salt and pepper shakers on the table. She did a survey of the scene; it looked nice with the red-and-white-checkered tablecloths, and though she had never been to Italy, it looked like the pictures she saw in the magazines. Italy was definitely at the top of her list of where she wanted to go, to take Italian cooking lessons there. "Dream on," Lizzy said to herself.

Lizzy waited patiently. She thought the service should have ended by now. Finally, a stream of people came in the front door. It seemed to Lizzy that the people sounded like happy little bees swarming. Lizzy announced to the people that the food was ready, where the drinks were, and the locations of the bathrooms. After the people sat down at the tables, they bowed their heads and prayed before they proceeded to eat. She thought in a world where there was hunger and starvation, maybe everyone should thank God for their food.

Brad came in and apologized, but he explained that after each service he asked people to come forward if they wanted to become a follower of Christ. He called it an "altar call." Brad looked at Lizzy and asked, "Who do you think came up with the idea to accept Christ?"

Lizzy was still reeling at the altar call part. "I am not sure—who?"

"Bonnie Spencer and David Smith!" Brad said, sounding like he had just hit the lottery. "They are with some of the deacons now. I am sure they will want to tell you their stories personally when they come in. I also want you to meet the Landrys from Oakmont. I told you they own Casey's restaurant. They said they wanted to meet a fellow restaurateur. Here they come now."

Brad introduced Michael and Cindy Landry. Lizzy was surprised at how nice they were. They complimented her cooking as they were sampling her pastas. They couldn't believe that they had never been to the pub before and apologized. But they thought Lizzy would understand because she knew owning a restaurant was an all-consuming business. They loved her pastas and told her that if she ever wanted to freelance and cater her pastas, they would be interested in talking about a business arrangement.

Lizzy realized that the Who's Who were the most unpretentious people she had ever met in her life. She shook their hands and told them, "Thank you, and I will certainly consider your offer." They shook Brad's hand, too, and told him they were very impressed with his sermon and would be back next week. They told him not to hesitate to call them if he needed any help.

Just then, Bonnie and David walked in, appearing drunk. Lizzy looked puzzled and asked them, "I thought you two were still in the church. Did you go to a VFW club next door?"

They both exploded with laughter. "No, we haven't had an ounce of alcohol. We literally feel like the weight of the world has been lifted off our shoulders. We feel like we are children again."

Lizzy was confused and relieved, but she was also happy because they were happy. She told them they had better go eat while there was still food left. She would catch up with them later.

Brad came over to Lizzy after telling the last few people to have a good day and said, "Thank you so much. This went great, and you orchestrated the whole thing perfectly." With that, he gave her a friendly hug. "Why don't we grab a bite to eat and sit with David and Bonnie?" he asked. The two had barely touched their food because they were talking so much. "I will help you clean up after we are done eating."

Lizzy felt like she was going to bust out of her seams with pride. "You are welcome, and I am starving and think that's a great idea. Let me grab a few sodas, and I will meet you at the table." Lizzy felt like she had just finished the race in first place. She was overjoyed with feelings of happiness and felt a great sense of accomplishment.

When Lizzy sat down with Bonnie, David, and Brad, she couldn't help but notice how bubbly they all were, talking about the feelings they were having. She couldn't relate or understand this energy they were suddenly feeling, but she sat there and listened.

Brad looked at Lizzy with affection, touching her hand and smiling to include her in the conversation, because he knew she was feeling left out. Toward the end of the meal, he asked Bonnie if she wanted him to come see her son, Tony, later that day.

"Yes, I would really appreciate that. But I am going to warn you, he is like a runaway train that is getting ready to crash."

"Don't worry, I have dealt with this before. I have found there might be deep-seated anger issues, but once they are addressed and resolved, kids can have an attitude change."

"That would be great if that's all it takes. But I just wanted to give you a heads-up. How about five o'clock today?"

Brad nodded. "Bonnie, don't worry. I am sure that he's not that far gone, and with God all things are possible. I will bring you a Bible when I come so it doesn't seem preplanned to Tony. Maybe you can take your other son, Ian, for a walk so that we can have a few moments alone."

Bonnie's happiness was diminished by worry, but she said she would pray for a miracle. They all got up. Brad told David that he would be by tomorrow night with his Bible, then he closed by saying, "Welcome to the family," as they walked out the door.

Brad then turned to Lizzy. "What now, captain?"

They spent a couple of hours cleaning up, breaking down the tables, and putting things back in their normal places. They both were excited about the outcome of the day and happily recapped the events. They should have been exhausted, but they were quite the opposite.

Brad kept feeling like he had known Lizzy a lot longer than a week, and he thoroughly enjoyed spending time with her. He said to himself, "I wish there were more than twenty-four hours in a day."

Brad left Lizzy with another hug, but before he could walk out the door, Lizzy handed him a piece of paper with her cell phone number on it. She asked, "If you don't mind, can you call me and tell me how things go with Tony? I am truly worried about Bonnie's situation with her son. From the stories she tells me, I am afraid he is heading toward juvenile court or even worse."

Brad replied, "I would be happy to do that. Try not to worry. Maybe it's not that bad yet. I will let you know what happened later on."

With that, Brad gave her another hug and left. Lizzy locked up and went upstairs to do her waiting paperwork.

CHAPTER 8

Brad Schmidt started his trip to see Bonnie and her son, Tony, about 4:45, because MapQuest said it would take only ten minutes to get to the address Bonnie had given him.

MapQuest directed him up Center Avenue to Fourth Street, located before entering Penn Hills, the surrounding borough to the east. He took a right and went a quarter of a mile. He found the house on the right, and he pulled in front of it and parked. He took a quick survey of the area, made up of modest cookie-cutter, brick Cape Cod houses. There were only a few that weren't in need of yardwork and painting. He said a little prayer for guidance before heading to the front door. He rang the doorbell and heard Bonnie yelling, "Get off that video game and go answer the door!"

The door opened, and there before Brad's eyes stood a tall, young teenager with black curly hair and dark eyes. He was wearing jeans that were pulled down so Brad could see the boxers he was wearing underneath.

Tony looked at Brad, and in a deep, harsh voice said, "What do you want?"

"Hello, I'm Brad Schmidt from the First Baptist Church of Verona. I am here to see your mom," Brad said with a smile on his face.

Tony quickly turned away as though he had seen a ghost and let Brad enter the home. Tony directed him into the kitchen, where Bonnie was preparing dinner. Her youngest son, Ian, was already sitting at the table, waiting for the arrival of his plate. There were two other plates sitting on the table. Brad assumed those plates were for her and Tony.

"Hi, Bonnie, I want to give you this gift, a Bible, for coming to church today."

"Wow, that is so nice of you. You didn't have to bring it all the way up here. I really appreciate it." She then handed the Bible to Ian to look at. She paused. "We are just getting ready to eat. Won't you join us? There is plenty to spare."

Brad wasn't at all hungry, especially for what looked like spaghetti, but he knew this was a hint from Bonnie, a hint to talk to Tony. "Sure, I would like that, if you are sure."

"Yes, I would be happy if you would join us. Tony, go get a chair from the living room. Then go wash your hands for dinner."

Tony let out a sigh in disgust, but he did as his mom had asked and sat down at the table. This was not what Brad had thought would happen, them all sitting and eating dinner together, but in his line of work, he had learned to improvise. Bonnie asked Brad to say grace before they ate, and again there was that sigh of disgust from Tony.

Brad couldn't help but notice that Tony was squirming in his seat. He never lifted his head to make eye contact with him, so Brad decided to ask some simple questions about school—did he play basketball because of his height, or did he have a girlfriend yet? Tony's responses were "yes" or "no." So Brad decided to get away from close-ended questions and ask him something open-ended that he would have to answer. He asked, "So, what things do you like to do?"

"I like to hang out with my friends. Is there a problem with that?" Tony said in a combative way.

"No, there is no problem with that, but your mom is concerned that your older friends may be taking you down the wrong path."

With that, Tony jumped up from the table. "Now I see what you are doing. I don't want or need your advice. You are not my father—that's because I don't have a father."

"No, you don't have a father, but you have a mother who loves and cares for you deeply. She is worried about you."

"Well, if she cared that much, she should have provided me with a dad." With that, Tony grabbed his jacket, which had the emblem of a rat on the back, and stormed out of the house.

Bonnie immediately apologized to Brad for her son's behavior and stated that was the norm for these days. She asked, "So, what do you think is going inside of that head of his?"

"Bonnie, I hate to say this, but this is a common occurrence with boys his age who don't have a dad or a strong male influence in their lives. They seek that relationship in older boys, and that is why so many gangs are so successful in recruiting young boys. They replace that void. I don't think Tony is at that point yet, but he certainly needs some redirection. I could feel the conflict in him, as though he knows it's wrong and his conscience is bothering him.

"Why don't you bring him to church next week? We have a lot of kids his age, and maybe introducing him to a different group of friends will give him the option to choose, and to see that there are other options available."

Brad hung around Bonnie's house for a while and played and talked to Ian. He could tell Ian felt like he was in the middle, because he loved both of them very much. Ian wished his brother would change and be his old self again.

Brad put on his coat and gave Bonnie and Ian a hug and left. Brad sensed there was trouble brewing, and he felt a deep concern for the whole situation. He prayed all the way home. The first thing he did when he got settled at his place was to call Lizzy.

"Hi, Lizzy, it's Brad."

"Hi, how did it go?"

"It didn't go very well. Tony stormed out of the house." He told her about all the details.

In the meantime, after Tony had made a scene with the 'Preacher Man,' he called his friends and told them to meet him up at the clubhouse, which really was a shed at the back of an abandoned warehouse. Pete and Kyle showed up, wearing matching rat emblems on the back of their jackets, and asked a bunch of questions.

Pete started, "Do you think he knows it was us who started the fire at his church?"

Tony replied, "I don't think so, but like I said at the time, I didn't think it was a good idea when you lit the match."

Kyle turned into the conversation. "Who cares? It's already done. What should we do tonight for some more fun?"

Pete answered, "Why don't we go into Penn Hills and steal a bike? Maybe we could sell it to one of those spoiled brats in Oakmont, or take it apart and sell it as parts?"

The red flags were going off again in Tony's head. He didn't think it was a good idea, but he didn't want to appear weak to his older friends, and so he agreed to go. They walked about a mile and spotted an unlocked bike leaning against a tree near a house, and they took it.

They took the bike back to the shed and agreed to meet again on Tuesday, after school, to walk it down to Oakmont to try to sell it. Little did they know that the house from which they had stolen the bike belonged to Victor Rodriguez, a reputed gang member of the Night Crawlers, and that the bike belonged to his little brother. The worst part was that Victor had placed cameras outside the house in case of trouble—he saw the whole thing on tape the next morning. Victor immediately called one of the members of his club to find out who and where the thieves were from.

After their initial conversation about Tony, Brad and Lizzy talked on the phone for hours about anything under the sun. Finally Brad suggested that it was already Monday and they had better get some shut-eye. Brad was attracted to the genuine concern Lizzy had for others, and he thought she had a great heart.

Before they disconnected the call, Brad asked Lizzy, "Would you like to go eat at Casey's next Sunday after the service, and then go across the river to Zone 28, the bowling alley? It's my treat this time."

"Yes, that sounds great."

"Great. I will be by tomorrow with your check for the buffet, and if it's Monday meat loaf, I'm staying," he said with a chuckle.

Lizzy laughed. "I must be predictable. I will see you tomorrow evening, I meant later today. Good night."

CHAPTER 9

On Monday morning the weather was cloudy. Their wakeup alarms came too early for both Lizzy and Brad. Brad had contractors who were showing up at 7 a.m. to hang new drywall. The whole interior of the church had to be gutted. Apparently, when drywall got wet, it became nonfunctional. So, all of it needed to be removed. All that was now left were the two-by-fours. It looked like the church was undergoing new construction in its early stages. Luckily, after they brought in huge fans and dehumidifiers, the kitchens, bathrooms, and electricity weren't damaged. So, today Brad's job was to oversee the contractors, and he needed to look at paint colors and new carpet. He had an understanding of what his dad must have gone through by trying to keep the costs down while building the church, and Brad had a new respect for him as well.

Lizzy, on the other hand, had to do paperwork, clean the pub, go to the bank, pick up a liquor order, be there for the delivery of the orders from Sysco and Fuhrer's

Beer Distributors, put those away, make meat loaf from the meat that was delivered, and finish the daily special, all before 2:00 p.m. So, when she rolled out of bed at 6 a.m., she said in a sluggish voice, "Let the games begin." Lizzy had grown up in the restaurant business and knew that one day was only twenty-four hours long, and no one day was similar to the next. Whatever happened, she knew change was on its way. It was this philosophy that kept her sane and moving forward.

Lizzy's day pressed on. She found herself looking at the clock when it turned 3:00. She opened the door of the pub and Bonnie was the first one again through the door. Lizzy thought she looked like death warmed over. Bonnie had worry written all over her face, and she looked sleep-deprived. Bonnie told Lizzy that it hadn't gone very well with her son Tony the night before. Lizzy told Bonnie that Brad had filled her in.

"Well, that was just half of it. Tony didn't come home until after midnight. I swear, I don't know if I am going to survive this. I prayed all night. I felt a little comfort, but I couldn't seem to shake the demons of worry out of my head."

Just then, Joe Russo came into the pub. He tried to comfort Bonnie, but she shook him off like a mosquito. They both suddenly walked out, and Lizzy could hear them arguing with each other as they walked down Arch Street.

Lizzy was wondering what that was all about, when Brad walked through the door.

"What's up? You look perplexed."

"Bonnie came in and was upset because Tony didn't come home until after midnight. Then Joe Russo came in to try to comfort her. She shook him off like a mosquito, but then they both stormed out in an argument. I could hear them shouting at each other all the way down Arch Street. I am not sure what that was all about, because I have never seen them disagree about anything before."

"Wow, that's too bad, but we shouldn't speculate. Bonnie will share if she wants to. I am, however, very concerned about Tony and whatever he was up to after midnight. I am afraid he was up to no good."

Lizzy looked forlorn and nodded in agreement. "Unfortunately I think you are right."

"I don't mean to change the subject, but here is your check." Brad handed it to her without an envelope.

"Why does this say three hundred dollars? I thought you said two hundred dollars."

"I know that is what we agreed upon, but I couldn't help but notice that you had furnished all the drinks, plates and such, and all the table decorations," replied Brad. He continued, "You shouldn't have to pay for that out of your own pocket. I am beyond grateful for all the effort and care you put into making the day better than

I could have imagined. So, it is only fair that the church pays for the rest."

Lizzy reluctantly accepted the check and put it into the cash register. Bonnie returned alone and announced that she and Joe were no longer friends. Lizzy could tell that she had been crying, but she felt like Bonnie somehow had taken back control of her life. It was a sense of empowerment, Lizzy thought, and in her mind, she was saying, "Way to go, Bonnie!"

Bonnie sat down. "I will have one of your blue plates and a Sprite."

Brad said, "Make that two." Brad told Bonnie that all they could do at the moment was to pray that Tony didn't go past the point of no return in man's laws. In God's laws, he could be forgiven in Christ no matter what he had done.

"So, what you are saying is that you hand Tony over to God, pray fervently, and trust that He will take care of it the way He sees best?"

"Exactly. That is what we call faith."

Lizzy brought two plates and two drinks over and told them to enjoy it. Brad asked Lizzy, "Can you join us?"

"I'd better not. I need to stand guard for the incoming people."

Brad laughed. "'Stand guard'? I think you missed your calling. You should have joined the army." All three of them broke out in laughter.

Brad finished his entire plate of food and paid for both his and Bonnie's. He also left a nice tip for Lizzy. "That was delicious, and thanks again," he said.

As he began to walk out the door, David walked in. Brad said, "Hi, David, I was hoping to see you. I wanted to hand-deliver this Bible to you personally and tell you that if you need anything or have any questions, I put my card on the front page."

David looked at the book as though he had been handed a million dollars.

"Thanks, Preacher. I really appreciate it." Surprisingly, David sat down next to Bonnie. He and Bonnie started a low-tone conversation. Lizzy couldn't hear what they were saying, but she could tell David was giving her compassionate counsel, because Lizzy could hear the words coming from Bonnie: "Thank you..." "It will be alright..." and "It was wrong from the beginning..." Lizzy thought, "Here sit two people whose lives have changed so dramatically, but they are taking care of each other." Lizzy thought for sure that she wanted whatever it was they had.

In the meantime, Tony was watching Ian as always after school, while his mom, he knew, was at the pub again. He was resenting that he was always put in charge of babysitting while other kids had a life. He had been getting bullied at school. The other kids were telling him he was an illegitimate son of Joe Russo's. He didn't know if that was true or not, but he had lost all respect for his mom. He felt unwanted and lonely, and he'd even considered running away.

Tony yelled at Ian, "Come on, let's go outside and play. It looks like Mom is going to be home late again. If she isn't back soon, I will fix you something to eat." He looked down at Ian's innocent face and thought, "It isn't your fault, either. We are both in the same boat."

Around dusk, a red car came barreling down the street. At the last second, Tony dove out of the way of the car—but Ian wasn't that quick and he stood in the road, looking like a deer caught in the headlights. The car struck Ian, and his little body was thrown onto the grass in front of their house. The car didn't stop, or even slow down as it sped away.

Tony's heart came up to his throat, and he couldn't believe his eyes. He ran over to Ian, who was crying and holding his leg. "Are you okay? Where are you hurt?" Tony asked in a concerned voice.

Ian screamed through his tears. "It's my leg! I want Mommy!"

Tony pulled his cell phone from his pocket and called his mom. As usual, she would had her phone off, so he instinctively called 911.

The ambulance arrived quickly, and the EMS technician asked Tony where his mom was. He told her that his mom was running some errands and he was babysitting for her, which wasn't true, but he didn't want to tell them she was at a pub.

They told Tony that Ian's leg was most likely broken and that they needed to transport him to UPMC in Fox Chapel. They told him he could ride along, but the police would definitely need more details about the hit and run and would probably come to the hospital as well.

They loaded Ian onto a gurney and into the ambulance. He was screaming in pain with every move. Tony jumped in behind them and watched as they put a temporary splint on Ian's leg. They said his vitals were good, but they would need to check for internal bleeding when they got to the hospital. Tony got his phone out while they were being transported and called the landline at the pub.

He could hear it ring, and then a woman's voice said, "Allegheny River Pub. This is Lizzy speaking."

"This is Tony. Is my mom there?"

"Yes, she is here. Do you want me to put her on the phone?"

"Yes!" Tony snapped. "Why else would I be calling?"

Lizzy knew something terrible must have happened because Tony never called the pub before. She summoned Bonnie to the phone. "It's Tony."

Lizzy couldn't hear the conversation, but Bonnie's face went void of color and her response was, "Oh my God, I will be right there."

Bonnie hung up the phone. "There was an accident. Ian apparently was hit by a car and is on his way to UPMC in Fox Chapel by ambulance. I need to go."

"I wish I could leave and drive you, but I will call Suzie Q and come over as quickly as possible," Lizzy exclaimed.

David stood up. "I can drive you. I haven't had anything to drink tonight." Bonnie agreed, and they both walked out, got into Bonnie's car, and drove off toward Fox Chapel, which was on the other side of the Allegheny River. They would have to cross the Hulton Bridge. It was about a fifteen-minute drive from the pub.

Lizzy got on the phone and called Suzie Q. "Suzie, can you come in and cover for me? There has been an accident involving Bonnie's son Ian. They are taking him to the hospital, and I think I should go be with her."

"Sure, we were just watching Dancing with the Stars anyway. I can have my husband Tivo it. Besides, this is much more important. I will be there in five."

CHAPTER 10

At the hospital, Ian had to go through a battery of tests such as X-rays, a CAT scan, and bloodwork. Tony stayed at his brother's side the entire time. They sedated Ian, and when Bonnie came into the ER cubical, he was asleep. She looked at Tony and asked, "What happened?"

Tony told his mom that they had been outside playing when a red car came barreling down the street, and it seemed like the driver hadn't seen them. He went step by step through his explanation.

Bonnie looked confused. "So, you were playing in the middle of the street?"

Tony replied, "No, we were by the curb."

Tony resented the fact that his mom was implying that the accident was somehow his fault. But the wheels in his head had been turning all evening as he replayed the accident in slow motion. Tony wasn't going to argue with his mom, because the car might not have seen them, but Tony couldn't be positive that the car wasn't coming at them on purpose. And although he hadn't gotten a real close look at the man's face, Tony was sure there'd been a smile on it. He kept going around in his head about the stolen bike, and he couldn't help but wonder if Ian's accident had something to do with it. So, maybe it was his fault. If it was, the guilt that had crept into his head wasn't going anywhere soon.

A Verona officer walked in and said, "Sorry to bother you. My name is Officer Lange. I have some questions about the accident. It's my understanding that this was a hit-and-run."

Bonnie said, "Sure, but I wasn't there. He was under the care of my son Tony here. I am sure he will tell you everything he knows. He told me that it happened so fast that he doesn't remember much."

"That's okay, ma'am. We need as much information as possible to try to find out who did this. So, I am going to ask your son a series of questions, such as his age, their location, and exactly what he saw and remembers, so we can make a report to be circulated to the department. Is that acceptable?" Bonnie nodded yes.

Tony told the officer what he remembered, but he left out the part about the stolen bike, so as not to incriminate himself. His answers were vague, so the interview was short. The police officer thanked them and left.

Bonnie and Tony were anxiously sitting in the ER room waiting for the doctor to tell them what was going on. A nurse checked in on Ian and told them the doctor should be in shortly, but that was the fourth time she had said that. When Lizzy finally came through the door and hugged Bonnie, she said, "Sorry, it took so long. A group of eight people walked into the pub right as I was getting ready to walk out. They, of course, wanted to try the blue plate meat loaf. I couldn't leave Suzie Q alone at that point. I knew that would be too much for CJ to handle."

"You don't have to apologize, sweet friend. I am just glad you are here now. We have been waiting for the doctor to come in and tell us what is going on. It seems like it is taking forever for that to happen," Bonnie anxiously said. Tony just sat there, looking down, not saying a word.

Just then a petite Asian woman came in wearing a white coat. "Hello, my name is Dr. Hu. I have some good news and some bad news. The good news is that except for a bruised spleen, there appears to be no internal bleeding. Which in this case may be a bit miraculous, because the velocity of the car must have been significant due to the damage to his right leg. That leg is the bad news: The femur has extensive damage and will require surgery. An orthopedic surgeon has been called. He will better describe exactly what he is going to do.

Usually in these cases, they place a rod in the leg with screws. But I think due to his age and the fact that he is not done growing yet, they may attach a frame outside his leg until the bone is healed. That means he will be at the hospital for three to five days, with another eight weeks in the frame and cast, followed by physical therapy. All in all, it will be at least six months for his total recovery."

The doctor continued, "Dr. Sweeny will be your orthopedic surgeon. He will tell you the particulars. He has scheduled your son's surgery for the first thing in the morning. The nurse will be in to explain the rest and what room in the hospital he will be admitted into. Like I said, it could have been worse. Your son looks like a healthy child, and he should make a total recovery."

Bonnie started sobbing after the doctor left the room. On the one hand, she was relieved, but the reality had kicked her in the face, knowing there was a long road ahead of them. She just kept repeating, "I can't believe this. But thank You, Lord, for not taking away my precious boy."

After her initial breakdown, she looked at Lizzy. "Do you think you could drive Tony home? There is no need for all of us to stay here and wait."

"Of course, I would be happy to do that. Do you want Tony to stay with me for a while?"

"Tony is responsible enough to go home and to get himself to school on his own. If I need you, I will let you know," Bonnie answered knowing what a problem her son could be. She didn't want to burden Lizzy with that.

Bonnie added, "David said he would get someone to help bring my car over and let me know where it is parked. So, I can pick Tony up and bring him over to the hospital after school tomorrow." Bonnie then looked Tony straight in the eyes, "Tony, I am sorry if you thought I was accusing you of this accident. I know it wasn't your fault, but sweetheart, I really need you to step up to the plate and be responsible. Can you do this for me and your brother?"

Guilt-stricken, Tony nodded his head. "You can count on me, Mom. I feel bad about the whole thing, even though it wasn't my fault. I promise I will get to school on time." Tony knew the first thing he was going to do when he got home was to call Pete and Kyle and tell them what had happened. He would ask them not to do anything with the bike until they figured out what was going on.

On the way to Bonnie's house, Lizzy tried to start a conversation with Tony, but she was shot down like a duck in flight during hunting season. She thought he was acting guarded, and she suddenly felt empathy for Bonnie. She wondered if this was the way Tony acted normally, and if so, no wonder Bonnie was stressed out.

Lizzy dropped Tony off at his house and arrived back at the pub a little before midnight to close the bar. Suzie Q was capable of closing up herself, but this made it a lot easier. Lizzy gave Suzie and Carlos a brief synopsis of what happened and said good night. Lizzy felt an urgency to call Brad. After some contemplation, she felt it was the right thing to do because she had heard somewhere that one of the pastoral duties was to visit the hospitals.

She dialed her phone, and a groggy Brad answered. "I am so sorry to bother you this late, but there was an accident tonight." She proceeded to tell him the whole story.

"You were right to call me. I will head to the hospital tomorrow to sit with Bonnie during Ian's surgery as support and comfort. What time is the surgery scheduled? Are you going to be there too?"

"The ER doctor said that the scheduled surgery would be the first thing in the morning, but I am not sure what time that meant. Yes, I was thinking for the same reasons as you that I will go over there tomorrow morning."

"I think 'early' means like seven to eight o'clock. I will probably go over at seven just in case Ian's first on the schedule. Do you want me to pick you up?"

"I think I'd better drive myself because I have a mountain of things I need to get done here too."

"Okay, I will see you in the morning, then. I will stop and pick up coffee and muffins from Oakmont Bakery on the way. Thanks again for calling. Good night."

Exhausted, Lizzy replied, "Thanks. Good night."

Brad walked into the surgery center waiting room at 7 a.m., where a washed out–looking Bonnie sat. She was so happy to see him. He told her that Lizzy had called him the night before and that she was on her way. He then handed Bonnie a bag with a muffin, as well as sugar and creamer for her coffee. When Lizzy walked into the room, Brad said a prayer before they ate, but mostly they prayed for Ian.

They waited there for close to three hours with a volunteer periodically coming out and giving them a progress report. They kept the conversation light to keep Bonnie out of the worry zone, and finally the surgeon came into the room.

"Hi, my name is Dr. Sweeny. I have some really good news concerning your son. The X-rays were erroneous, and the severity of the break wasn't as bad as it looked on the films, which in itself is a rarity. Also, the break was clean, and there didn't seem to be any damage to the nerves or muscles surrounding the break in his leg, which is also somewhat miraculous. So, I put four screws into the bone, and then after sewing him up, I placed a frame to the screw, setting the bone together. Then, I casted up to his thigh. If there aren't any complications, such as infection, he should be able to go home in three days. I make my rounds at six in the morning, so if you have any questions, be in his room at that time. I believe that even though there is still a long process of healing, your son should have no physical repercussions from this. He should make a full recovery except for the scar."

Bonnie couldn't thank the doctor enough. "God bless you," she told the doctor as he walked out of the room. Brad, Lizzy, and Bonnie were so relieved that they started laughing, smiling, and hugging each other. They couldn't believe how the doctor's report was so good. Although Brad didn't say it, he could see God's hand in this, because he had seen miracles before. He would bring that up at a later date, but for now he just said, "Thank God!"

Bonnie insisted that Brad and Lizzy should go on their way, that she could handle the rest. Brad told her if there was anything that he could do, he would be glad to help. He informed her that the contractors weren't scheduled to come until the next day. Bonnie gave a pause and asked, "Actually, do you think you could pick up Tony after school and bring him over to the hospital?"

"I can do that. What time does he get home?"

"He gets home at four o'clock, and I will text him to make sure that he will be there. I think he is feeling bad, so I don't think he will be giving me any trouble—at least for a little while."

"I will be there a little early. Do you want me to pick him up some chicken nuggets and a soda?"

"That would be great. I don't think there will be any snacks at the house, because I usually go to the store today."

Brad and Lizzy walked out together, both relieved, and decided they would call each other later to get updates about Ian, but mostly they really just wanted to talk to each other.

CHAPTER 11

Brad showed up at Bonnie's house about ten minutes early to pray for wisdom on how to deal with Tony. He had counseled some prodigal kids before, but he realized Tony was more wayward than the others he had dealt with in the past.

Just then Tony walked down the street with his earbuds in. Brad jumped out of the car with two bags of food and drinks and a big smile. "Do you want to eat before we go to the hospital?"

Tony gave a half-hearted smile, took off his earbuds, and opened the door to let both of them in. Tony had gotten the text from his mom, and he was extremely agitated by the fact that the preacher was coming to pick him up. He decided he'd better toe the line for now and so he said, "Thank you," when Brad handed him the food.

"Let's eat here before we go because I don't like fast food in my car." Really what Brad was hoping was that he could break through Tony's tough exterior get to the root of what was really bothering him.

"So, your mom probably told you that Ian was very lucky. He looks to make a full recovery. I hope you're not beating yourself up, thinking it was your fault."

Tony thought Brad seemed genuinely nice, and he felt an overwhelming conviction, like he was carrying so much weight that he was going to break. Tony imagined that he was outside of his body looking in, and he thought, "Who is that young punk sitting there, and where did he go wrong?" Tony really didn't like the person he had become. He wanted desperately to escape, but he didn't know how.

Brad asked sincerely, "Do you think it was an accident?" At that point, Tony came unglued. He thought Brad could see right through him and knew the truth. Tears came streaming down his face.

"I am so tired of the lies. I'm so sorry about everything, and I wish I could take all of it back." Tony sobbed out the words. Then Tony came clean about everything: how he had been with Pete and Kyle the night Pete struck the match at the church and he didn't do anything about it. About the night they stole the bike. How Tony didn't know if the accident was a retaliation for the stolen bike, but the coincidence haunted him.

Brad went over to Tony and gave him a hug. Tony thought he should have given him a well-deserved slap in the face. Brad explained about forgiveness. Jesus told us that God will forgive us all if we repent, accept Jesus, and turn back to Him. This is free because Jesus paid the fine for all of our sins on the cross. Brad asked Tony, "Do you want something free that will change your life—which you obviously don't like—and allow you to have a fresh start?"

"Are you kidding? Yes, I do."

Brad prayed the salvation prayer with Tony as he cried like a baby. Tony felt something he had never experienced before. It felt like pure, peaceful power entered his body, and he knew for sure that he was forgiven.

After his crying subsided, he asked, "But what about the bike and church?"

Brad replied, "Where is the bike now?"

"It's up the hill at our hangout."

"We are going to go and get it right now, then take the bike back to where you stole it from and apologize. I think I can smooth things out, but you will need to promise that you won't ever do anything like that again. I don't think we can prove that they hit your brother, but they will fear that the police could get involved and so they will let it rest. As far as the church arson, I need for you and your friends to come to the church tomorrow after school and for some time after that to help paint it. If your friends don't want to help repaint the church, remind them about their future in the courts. I am only giving one free pass. They should take it if they are smart. Let's get going so we can get to the hospital. I think you should tell your mom when the time is right. You will know when."

Tony felt like for the first time he had not only hope, but he felt like he had a big brother mentor in Brad. He definitely wanted to know more about Jesus, who had come to his rescue.

Brad and Tony went to the clubhouse and retrieved the bike. They took it to Victor's house. The beginning of the word exchange was volatile, when Victor first came out of his house carrying a gun. But by the end, there was a meeting of the minds and a warning to both sides to stay off each other's turf. Brad felt confident that they were never going to see each other again and that this chapter was closed forever.

As Brad and Tony went to the hospital, all Tony could do on the way was to thank Brad. "Don't thank me. Thank God. He is in control now."

When they walked into the hospital room, Bonnie was sitting on a chair next to a sleeping Ian. She asked about their lateness. Brad explained that they had had a long talk and that Tony had volunteered to paint the interior of the church. He was also going to try to get his friends Pete and Kyle to volunteer as well.

Bonnie's face looked at Brad with an expression that seemed to say, Are we talking about my son? She could tell something was different about Tony when he came in with a smile and hugged her.

Brad made his excuses and left, knowing that Tony was in a brand-new chapter of his life. He could tell Tony was excited to tell his mom the whole story, thus opening that chapter in a new and deeper mother-and-son relationship.

Brad called Lizzy as he was crossing the Hulton Bridge. "I am heading your way. There is too much to tell you over the phone." Brad hadn't had time to eat his bag of food. He was hungry and asked, "What are the blue plate specials for tonight?"

"Vegetable soup and a 'hamburger in paradise' with fries."

"That's my second favorite meal," he said with a chuckle. "I will be there in less than fifteen minutes," and he ended the call.

Lizzy gave out an excited sigh and proceeded into the kitchen to prepare, with a lot of TLC, a blue plate special for Brad while thoughts of him darted back and forth in her head.

Brad came in and sat down next to Teddy Summer. Brad had thought on the way there that the people of the pub were exactly the people who needed to hear the "good news." He needed to go out to find the lost because that's what Jesus had said about making disciples of "all" people—not just the ones who came to church.

Brad gave Lizzy a huge smile and a hug. "I can see you're super busy right now. Let's talk when things slow down. I am so excited to tell you about today. I am not going anywhere soon."

Lizzy was happy to hear those words, and deep inside wished he would stay forever. From 6 till 9 p.m., the pub was extremely busy for Lizzy. Apparently, word got out that Lizzy's jumbo wings and sauces were to die for, and she went through most of a forty-pound box of wings. She would have to get two boxes delivered ASAP from Sysco.

Brad talked to Teddy Summer, who seemed to have a ton of questions. He started at the beginning with creation versus evolution because if he didn't understand that, he wasn't going to get the rest. Brad couldn't help noticing that the three amigos from Daily's were eavesdropping. Brad was hoping he was planting some seeds in their heads too.

After the crowd dwindled down, Brad finally went to the table near the window. Brad told Lizzy about Tony's transformation. He didn't tell her about the stolen bike and the church arson, because he felt that was part of the confidentiality of his job as a pastor. He did, however, tell her that Tony and his friends were going to help paint the church. He added that they probably weren't going to need any insurance money, especially with the Landrys' donation.

Lizzy raved about what a brilliant person he was. She didn't want to appear too mushy and so she dialed it down a notch, but she really wanted to give him a big hug and a kiss. Little did she know that he was feeling the same way.

Lizzy declined Brad's offer to stay and help clean up, because she had Carlos there. Brad decided it was time to call it a day and headed back to his apartment, which was now stripped down to the studs. He had a deep feeling of accomplishment as he felt the Holy Ghost blessing him.

CHAPTER 12

The next day, Tony and his friends Pete and Kyle came after school to the First Baptist Church as promised. Brad sat the other two boys down and gave them an analogy about two paths. One path led to where there was everything that they would want. Brad used up-to-date examples like the "new PlayStation 4," "expensive cars," and "money." The other path led to "sewage," "puke," and "horrible pungent smells." He asked them which path they would take. Of course, they chose the first path. Brad told them those paths were examples of good versus evil, Jesus versus Satan, and he told them they were currently on the second path. Pete and Kyle didn't buy in to the Jesus thing yet, but they did buy in to the good path, and they agreed to make restitution by painting the church every day after school as payment, which in their minds beat the alternative of going to jail.

Brad gave them a lesson in Interior Painting 101 and got them started. He put Tony in charge of the project, citing the fact that it was his brother who could have been killed. He really wanted to build Tony's confidence as a leader, not a follower. After feeling confident they were doing a decent job, Brad went into the office and looked at the carpet swatches that he had picked up earlier that day. He was confused about which to choose and thought he would ask Lizzy. He really respected her opinion and was developing strong feelings toward her. He felt their friendship growing exponentially and was extremely happy about it.

The boys were on track all week, so Brad said they could take the weekend off, but that they must come back on Monday. Tony had already displayed an attitude adjustment. Pete and Kyle were not quite as adjusted as Tony. However, they let their guards down and looked at Brad as though he was their big brother. They were definitely showing signs of improvement.

The rest of the week Brad and Lizzy talked on the phone as if they were boyfriend and girlfriend. Brad went to the pub every night for the special. He showed Lizzy the carpet swatches, and she told Brad about a discount carpet place in Monroeville, a town east of Verona. Lizzy drove Brad to where she knew they had great prices. They picked a neutral-colored, commercial-grade carpet for half the cost of the ones he had previously selected. He was not only grateful but immensely enjoyed Lizzy's company.

The pub's business increased significantly, and Lizzy was able to add to her savings account, which had been scraping the bottom, at the minimum amount, the amount where it wasn't subject to a service charge. She was even thinking of adding on a waitress when Bonnie's salon girls, Crystal and Maggie, said they would alternate nights and work just for tips until Lizzy was able to hire someone full-time. Lizzy was impressed with the girls. Not only did they come every night, as promised, but they did a bang-up job waitressing. They received handsome tips for their good work. Crystal actually had gotten a date out of it from one of the guys in a nice group from Daily Juice, whom she served. Lizzy was hoping this was the nice guy that Crystal was looking for.

Sunday morning was a beautiful, warm and sunny day. Lizzy was looking forward to church, but more so for her first official date with Brad that afternoon after church. She got dressed into a stylish red and black sweater and black corduroys and prettied herself up by putting on makeup and lipstick. She walked downstairs at ten thirty to open the garage door. Brad walked in shortly after that.

"Good morning, sunshine," Brad said with a chirping voice.

Lizzy replied, "Good morning. It is a beautiful sunny morning."

Brad let out a hearty laugh. "I should have said you are like the sunshine."

Lizzy was sure she blushed because her face turned warm. "Thank you," she said and quickly changed the subject. "How many people do you expect today? I bet you noticed that the number doubled last week."

"Yes, I did notice that the numbers increased. It's just another example of how God can turn something bad into something good when He is involved in it."

"That's something I wanted to talk to you about. I have been giving some serious thought about making a commitment to Jesus. I know I must have sinned in my life, like taking pens from the bank and then some. Does this mean everything is covered by Jesus and that my name is written down in a book to go to heaven?"

Brad gave Lizzy a huge hug. "Yes, you are exactly right, and I am overjoyed with happiness that you have decided to do this. I can promise you that you will never regret it. You won't lose anything but gain everything." Brad then gave her a stronger warm hug that lasted much longer than the first hug. Brad added one more layer of affection toward Lizzy in that very minute, which was already growing by leaps and bounds.

People started to come into the Pub Pews church at a steady pace. Much to Lizzy's surprise, Teddy Summer came in and sat next to her. Then, if that weren't enough, Carlos and his family walked in, followed by

Suzie Q and her family. The cherry on top was when Bonnie and David walked in with her son Tony. The fashionable Landrys came as well, and several new faces. Lizzy couldn't do a head count because she was sitting near the front, but she felt like there was an increase again over the previous week. Lizzy thought the word was finally out about what a good preacher Brad was. It also meant the donations were increasing. Brad placed a box with a shot on the top with the word "Donations" on the side of the box by the pub's door. Lizzy didn't think it was any of her business, but she placed a fifty-dollar bill in it before he showed up. Brad didn't talk too much about donations except to tell the people that they should follow scripture and let the Holy Spirit direct their hearts on what to give. Lizzy found out later that 10 percent was customary.

The service this time started with a young man with an acoustic guitar. He played "I Can Only Imagine," by MercyMe, which Lizzy had never heard before. It talked about how when we die, what we would do when we first meet Jesus. Lizzy couldn't help but notice that there weren't any dry eyes in the pews, including hers.

The sermon that Brad eloquently presented was about a prophet in the Old Testament named Isaiah, who had predicted over seven hundred years before exactly how Jesus would come and die. It came to Lizzy's mind that God must have always had a plan to bring

His Son to earth all along, and He used this Isaiah to tell so that people during Jesus' time would believe when they read Isaiah's scrolls. She couldn't wait to dive into the Bible to learn everything there was to learn. Lizzy was both nervous and excited about the "altar call." She was looking forward to going to the front toward the end of the service.

The time had come for the altar call. She walked to the front and knelt, and much to her surprise she was not alone. David, Bonnie, and Tony knelt in support next to her on the pillows they had laid across the front pews. Next to her were Teddy and Carlos's wife with him by her side, but there were more unfamiliar faces, too, with other people standing behind, laying hands on them, in support. Lizzy thought they must be the deacons that Brad talked about. Lizzy resisted the habit she had to count everybody and instead closed her eyes and went to this moment. Brad first prayed for the needs that people had given him but also for Ian, Ian's family, and for his quick recovery. Brad prayed for them and then asked the people kneeling in the front to pray along with him. The summary of the prayer was to repent, turn away from sinning, let Jesus into their hearts, and follow Jesus. Lizzy considered herself a blameless geek, yet the tears came anyway when she thought of the things that she had done in the past. Then, there was an indescribable peaceful power, as though something just shot into her body. She found out later that it was the Holy Spirit's indescribable peace and love.

Brad looked at her as she knelt in front of him, and he could tell that she had received the Holy Spirit as it entered her. He thought of her as a breath of fresh air, and he was so excited that she had come to be a follower of Christ. He felt that way about everyone who became saved, that it was a spectacular event, but he became overcome by emotion with Lizzy's transformation. He truly felt love toward her and the notion that they weren't evenly yoked evaporated.

When it was all done, Lizzy understood why she had thought Bonnie and David were drunk before. She couldn't really find the words, but it felt like her feet weren't touching the ground; every tethered weight and worry was totally gone. She finally snapped out of her dazed state when she looked over and discovered everyone was gone except the Landrys, who were just getting ready to walk out. Lizzy could hear Brad tell them he would see them soon. Brad strolled over to Lizzy, with a grin from ear to ear, and said, "Are you ready to go?" He continued and said, "We have a lot to talk about. I want to know every detail of what you feel and think." Lizzy just nodded her head, because even those kind words of concern were making her emotional.

Brad and Lizzy arrived at Casey's just before one o'clock. It was still crowded but not packed, and the

Landrys had a "reserved" table for them. She looked at Brad with a smile and said, "You must know some people." They both decided to have breakfast instead of lunch and ordered the western omelet with hash browns, whole wheat toast, coffee, and tomato juice.

The order was hand-delivered by Cindy Landry. They thanked her, then Cindy said, "Do you have a minute?" They agreed and insisted that she sit down with them.

Cindy immediately asked Lizzy, "I know this is last minute, but is there any way you could prepare what you did last week for the buffet? I hesitate to ask, but our Italian chef went off and quit on me today. We are closed here tomorrow. So, I could pick up the ingredients, bring them to the pub, and then I can stay and help you cook them. This can be temporary while I find a replacement chef, or if it works out, we could make it permanent." Cindy continued in a desperate voice, "Please say yes."

Lizzy was totally caught off guard, but she didn't hesitate to say yes. She would add Suzie Q to the schedule and see if both Crystal and Maggie could come in as well.

Cindy jumped up and almost knocked a passing waitress's tray out of her hands. She excitedly said, "God bless you, Lizzy! You have no idea how you saved my day. Your meals are on me. When can I call you, Lizzy?"

"We are going over to Zone 28 to bowl after we eat. We shouldn't take too long because of all the strikes I am about to get." After they laughed, Lizzy went on, "How about eight o'clock tonight? Here's my cell number."

Brad looked at Lizzy. "Look at the chain of events. It's as though God is opening doors for you before your very eyes."

"I know one thing for sure—since I met you, my life has changed for the best, and I am so thankful that you are a part of it." She looked up and locked into his blue eyes, then kissed him. Brad felt like a high voltage spark had penetrated him during the kiss, something he had never felt before.

They went to the bowling lanes in Harmarville. Lizzy wasn't sure if she had been out of line to give him that kiss, but she figured it was as good a time as any to find out what Brad's intentions really were. She made good on her predictions of strikes—and she found out that the kiss she'd offered was like a Pandora's box. He obviously felt the same and kissed her after every strike. By the tenth frame of the third game, they had talked enough to make an "official" proclamation to become boyfriend and girlfriend, and they decided they would make each Sunday after church their "official date day."

They both agreed their whole worlds had revolved around Verona for too long, and it was time to step out of their boundaries and explore the rest of Pittsburgh.

They thought it would be fun if they took turns deciding the destination for the day. Brad, being the gentleman that he was, gave Lizzy the first turn to pick the date's spot.

Later that night, Cindy and Lizzy had finalized Monday over the phone. Lizzy couldn't sleep; she was in a total overload, but this overload was the best one she had ever had in her life. She must have replayed the day a dozen times in her head before she finally dozed off to sleep.

CHAPTER 13

Lizzy hadn't gotten out of bed yet, but she was thinking how her life had changed so dramatically since she'd met Brad. She still felt apprehensive and cautious because she wasn't sure if this was long-term or because her job just made her that way. She tried to put any negative thoughts away, but they lingered like the smell of sautéed onions and garlic.

Her Monday routine had changed since she'd agreed to help Cindy with her Italian dishes. Since she was going to make Italian dishes for Cindy, she decided to make extra Italian for the pub. She had gotten up in the middle of the night because she couldn't sleep, and so the pub was already clean, including the deep fryer.

After Lizzy finished her paperwork, she got the deposit ready, ate her toad-in-the-hole breakfast, then she decided to go to the bank early, as well as pick up the pub's liquor order. Cindy was scheduled to come at eleven, so that left Lizzy enough time to do the prep work for the sauces.

Cindy showed up right at eleven, dressed a little more casually than usual, but she still looked like she had just stepped out of a Macy's ad. Lizzy thought she would ask Cindy to go with her to upgrade her own wardrobe, since her clothes hadn't been replaced in years, and there was now a need for some special attire since she was dating Brad. Lizzy knew Cindy could improve her fashion sense.

"Good morning, Cindy!" Lizzy said with a smile as she let her into the pub.

"Good morning! Are we ready for some fun?"

Lizzy laughed because of what she would have said. They proceeded into the kitchen and flipped on the lights. "I already cut up the onions and garlic. I will grab the rest of the ingredients from the bags that you brought in, then let the games begin."

"Wow, Lizzy, do you ever sleep? How was your first date with Brad?"

"The date went fabulous, and we have decided to continue dating and see where it goes. And no, I couldn't sleep as a result of that. I couldn't get my wheels to stop turning. We decided to make Sunday our official date day, and we'll take turns choosing the destination."

"Oh, Lizzy, I'm so happy for you. Michael and I are really fond of Brad. I know you don't know this, but I am the daughter of a preacher. We are called PKs, which stands for 'preacher's kids.' Brad reminds me so much of my dad, who was very charismatic. He pastored Oakmont Presbyterian Church on Pennsylvania Avenue. My dad struggled at first to get people to attend, but by the end of his life, there were over five thousand members and three church services. That's why, when we saw the newscast about the fire, we prayed and definitely knew God wanted us to help."

"I am very fond of Brad, too but I'm embarrassed to seem so naïve. I am afraid to ask him questions. Since I just started my walk with the Lord, I am not sure how to express what I am feeling when I pray."

"Lizzy, just think of yourself as a baby in this new journey. It will take time for you to grow. Realize that the Bible and your prayers are milk for your soul, and the more you take in, the more you will grow. Eventually, with the help of the Holy Spirit, you will know because you will feel it from the inside out, and that's when you know for sure that it is right."

"But how will I know it is not my desires that make it seem so real?"

"Once you start to grow, you will be able to discern between what is God's will and yours. If I have any doubts, I always ask myself, 'What would Jesus do?'"

"I really appreciate your insight, Cindy. Thanks."

"Brad would have said the same. Set up time to read the scriptures every day. I would suggest starting in the New Testament, in the book of John. It really is a journey, but remember that Jesus paved the way. Stay focused, and you will find the way as well."

With that, they began cooking. Lizzy asked Cindy about clothing styles since her closet was full of jeans and oversized shirts. Cindy said she would love to take Lizzy shopping.

"Where are you going to go this week on your date?"

"I'm not sure. Do you have any suggestions?"

"Have you ever been to the Andy Warhol Museum on the Northside, downtown?"

"No, to be honest, I haven't been anywhere except the Strip District. I have been chained to this place."

"Try that one first. It's not too big, but there's a very interesting story about the eccentric Andy Warhol. His life and death were quite unusual and will result in some good conversation for you and Brad."

"Sounds like a good plan."

They finished preparing the dishes, and Cindy loaded her car with the trays of the Italian meals to take back to Casey's. She hugged Lizzy. "I really had a good time. I feel like I have known you a lot longer. I look forward to Thursday, when we go to the mall for some new clothes for you."

Brad and Lizzy talked every day on the phone about what was going on that day in their lives. He came to the pub on Wednesday night to try the jumbo wings.

He had heard everyone talking about how delicious they were.

"Where do you get wings this big? How do you cook them? I really like the garlic butter coating, because I'm not too fond of hot sauces."

Lizzy giggled, thinking to herself again that she liked how he could string together a list of questions like that. "They are from Sysco and come in a forty-pound bag. I used to order two boxes, but since I met you, I have my order up to four boxes. Thanks. I know they are big—some of the patrons call them 'pterodactyl wings.'"

Brad gave a hearty laugh. "I'm not sure they're quite that big, but boy, they are yummy."

Cindy took Lizzy to the Galleria at Pittsburgh Mills on Thursday, and Lizzy bought two new outfits. Cindy had suggested earth tones for Lizzy's complexion, so she bought an outfit at Macy's that consisted of brown corduroys, a matching sweater, and fashionable brown boots that were on sale. They also picked out an outfit at JC Penney's of khaki corduroys and a hunter-green and brown blouse with a vest. They cackled like high school friends throughout the shopping experience.

Lizzy decided to wear the Macy's outfit first, for today's church service and date. Sunday was a mixture of rain and snow, but it was expected to turn to all rain as the temperatures rose. Brad walked into the makeshift church that everyone now referred to as the "Pub Pew Church" and gave Lizzy a huge kiss and a hug.

"Wow! You look beautiful, Lizzy. Is that a new outfit?"

Lizzy told him about the shopping spree that she and Cindy had had on Thursday. She told him that she really enjoyed Cindy's company. She felt like they were developing a friendship, almost sisterly.

"I know what you mean, Lizzy. I felt blessed the minute I met the Landrys because they are such great ambassadors for the Lord."

"I know, Brad. I am not sure why some people think Christians have three heads, because it is totally not true. They are so caring and genuine."

"So, what plans have you made for us today?"

"I want it to be a surprise. I think you will like it, though. At least I hope so."

"I am sure whatever you decide to do will be great— just like you."

Brad got all his notes and placed them on his pulpit for the sermon. Lizzy sat in the back because the accountant in her liked to take inventory, in this case a people count. Really, it did her heart good to see new faces coming in. She counted 103, including herself, today.

After everyone was situated, the young woman with a guitar who was sitting on a stool at the front facing the congregation, said, "This song is from Kim Walker Smith, and it is called 'How He Loves Us'."

Lizzy had never been exposed to Christian music before, but she felt like there was something penetrating and magical about it. The music seemed to open up her heart and mind to be receptive to the message, and it stirred something deep inside of her.

Brad's sermon was from the book of 1 John, which was different from the book of John she had begun to read. Lizzy didn't know exactly where it was located, so she looked at the table of contents in her new Bible. She liked that she could maneuver around the Bible a lot better now that she was starting to read it every day.

Brad discussed six reasons why we need to connect to Jesus, including the fact that God wants us to experience His unconditional love, joy, forgiveness, and truth. He wants us to love again and face the future with confidence. God is with us, and Jesus showed us exactly how to do these things.

Lizzy felt the words Brad preached were what she needed to hear, and she could totally relate to them today. Maybe it wasn't as hard as she thought it would be. Something that Cindy had said earlier about being on a journey resonated with Lizzy. She was starting to see that coming to fruition for her, and if the journey was this great at the beginning, she was looking forward to a long, enjoyable one.

The service ended with a few people coming up for the altar call, and at one fifteen, they were ready to go. They got in Lizzy's car, she plugged in the address on MapQuest, and off they went. They pulled into the Andy Warhol Museum's parking lot on Sandusky Street, Northside, Pittsburgh, and parked.

"I have always wanted to come here, Lizzy. I have heard so many stories about him, and now I can find out if any of them are true. I love this—and I love you."

"I know I have wondered about him, too. I have to admit, this was Cindy's suggestion, so I can't take all the credit. We are first going to walk over to a restaurant called Mullen's Bar and Grill, on Federal Street. It has been in business for fifty years, which is always a good sign. It also got great reviews, and their hamburgers are supposedly superb. Is that okay?"

"Yes, you know how I like hamburgers."

When they walked into the restaurant, their first impression was that it looked like the pub, except it was totally covered in Pittsburgh sports paraphernalia. The wait staff all wore jerseys from Pittsburgh's different teams.

They both ordered hamburgers, fries, and Sprites. They probably should have split the half-pound burger because neither of them could finish their food. The hamburgers were great, and the conversation was equally great. They walked back to the museum, where a guided tour was just beginning.

The tour guide said they were going to start at the underground, where there was a conservation lab, the first floor was the entrance and gift shop, the second floor held the temporary exhibition hall, which now was displaying *The Chelsea Girls Exploded*, the third floor held the Archives Study Center, the fourth floor was dedicated to the 1980s, the fifth floor was dedicated to the 1970s, the sixth floor was dedicated to the 1960s, and seventh floor held an exhibit called *The Early Years*. They also would go into a room called *Andy Warhol's Silver Clouds*, which was a visual display of silver shapes floating around. Their hands fell together and stayed that way for the rest of the tour.

Brad and Lizzy knew about Warhol pop art and that he had created the Campbell's soup can labels, the Coca-Cola logo, the Monroe diptych, Orange Prince, and Warhol's various films. But they didn't know he was a devout Catholic. They also didn't know that in 1968, a woman named Valerie Solanas went to Warhol's hangout in New York called the Factory, and shot him. Warhol had theoretically died until they revived him. He also was said to have had a premonition about hospitals that created such a fear that he wouldn't go until his gallbladder was in bad shape. He died a couple of days after the surgery remove the gallbladder, from cardiac arrest, making his premonition come true.

Lizzy and Brad talked the whole way back to Arch Street about the museum, and what they liked or didn't like about it. They both agreed the first of their official date days had been perfect. They were already looking forward to the next one. Brad told Lizzy he would be over both Monday and Tuesday for dinner for her delicious specials. Before he got out of Lizzy's car, they kissed for a long time, and then they told each other good night.

CHAPTER 14

The pub seemed even more than a burden to Lizzy now that dating had become a part of her already-busy schedule. It was successful for her, but it involved less sleep, because she would clean the pub after midnight on Saturdays. She didn't know how long she could continue this pace, but she felt it was very much worth it. She genuinely felt that she and Brad both were falling in love with each other, but deep down, she couldn't help but think that love might not be enough. There was a tinge of disbelief that anything this good could really be happening to her, and she was holding on tight to her ace-of-heart card.

Lizzy did her usual Monday morning paperwork and deposits, as the sun from the east hit the treetops. She was feeling a bit overwhelmed, thinking about what lay ahead for the day, but she kept telling herself to take one step at a time.

Over at the church, Brad had a full schedule of work as well. Tony, Pete, and Kyle were still painting the walls, and Brad had painted the ceiling. He had to wash the half-moon stained-glass window in the front of the church, recaulk around it, then tape and cover around it, before the boys could paint the surrounding areas.

Brad had bought a twenty-foot teletron that another church was getting rid of. He thought it would be a good idea to install one for the people who sat at the back of the church. That had been a common complaint from the people, of not being able to see the front. Getting it to work was easier said than done, though. He eventually figured it out, and he would be ready for the reopening, scheduled for May third. The carpet and flooring were scheduled to come in the week before that. Brad prayed continually that there wouldn't be a problem with the last pieces of the puzzle.

Cindy showed up at the pub at eleven. She and Lizzy always enjoyed their conversations. They had somehow gotten on the subject of Cindy's mom. She said being a PK was nothing in comparison to being the wife of a preacher. "Being a preacher's wife isn't just sitting there looking pretty. She would go to the hospitals, arrange food for the wedding receptions held in the basement and the food for after the funerals. She organized Bible studies, and so much more."

Cindy went on, "That's why I didn't want to marry a preacher. But Mom loved what she did, and I never heard her complain. Of course, the restaurant business, I found out, is equally busy or worse."

Lizzy told Cindy all about their date to the Andy Warhol Museum. She thanked her for the suggestion. Lizzy told her that Brad was to plan next week's date, and she was very curious to find out where they were going to be going. Cindy gave Lizzy a big hug and told her to enjoy the rest of her day as she drove away.

Lizzy wrote on the erase board: "Ziti Marinara with a salad and bread." The pub was ready right on schedule, so she unlocked the door at three o'clock.

Bonnie was no longer the first one through the doors. She and David had become a couple, and now they waited until Tony and his friends came home from school, so they could take them over to the church to paint. They would show up later at four thirty, but now they only drank sodas. Then Brad would bring the boys down at six o'clock, and they would all sit together for dinner, after they said grace. Lizzy loved this routine much better, and she was so happy that there was finally harmony in their family.

The word was out about Lizzy Italian culinary skills, so the place was hopping for dinner. She wouldn't be able to join her friends and Brad for dinner, except for a quick soda, then back to work. During one of her mini-breaks, they collectively had decided to purchase tickets for the Pittsburgh Pirates' opening game against the

Cincinnati Reds for Thursday, April second, at one thirty-five, and they wanted to know if she was in. She used to go to the games with her dad and Vickie when she was little, but she hadn't been in at least twenty years. She gladly agreed to their plans of going to the game.

Finally, around eight o'clock, the rush was over, and she could sit with Brad, who was working on his sermon for Sunday. He was sitting by the window when Lizzy brought over a small plate of pasta for herself.

"So, are you going to tell me what we are going to be doing on Sunday?"

Brad chuckled. "Patience is a virtue, Lizzy. Haven't you ever heard that?" Brad wanted to tell her that he was going to take her to a fancy restaurant, but he enjoyed the playfulness of their interactions.

"Ha-ha. Can you at least tell me what I should wear?"

With a big smile, he said, "Yes. Wear something dressy."

"'Dressy'? What does that mean?"

"Like, a dress," he said while he held her hand affectionately.

"Really? I don't own one, but I enjoyed shopping with Cindy—so, new dress here we come!" They both broke out in laughter,

Brad had come over on Tuesday again for dinner, the meat loaf, but he couldn't get to the pub any more the rest of the week. That didn't bother Lizzy—she, too, was busy—and besides that, they would spend a considerable amount of time talking on the phone.

Lizzy thought Sunday arrived like the blink of an eye. She and Cindy had gone back to the mall, where they found a sweet floral dress with a matching button-down cardigan and she bought her first pair of high heels. Lizzy was wobbly at first in the heels, but soon she figured it out by walking a lot slower and picking up her feet.

Brad walked into the Pub Pews and looked at Lizzy. "You look absolutely beautiful. Lizzy Murphy, I believe you have outdone yourself. Wow."

Beaming with pride, Lizzy said, "Thank you, sweetheart."

Brad went up to the pulpit and placed his notes on it, along with his Bible. It wasn't much longer until the people started to file in. Today's singers were a couple named Peggy and John, and they sang a duet called, "You Are Faithful," by Skybird. They used a large karaoke machine as their instruments, and everyone sang along because the words were displayed on the screen. Lizzy was taken aback by the beauty and, again, the power that she felt in the words of the song.

Brad thanked the couple, then followed with a prayer and then the sermon. He asked everyone to turn to Deuteronomy 32:3–4, in the Old Testament. Lizzy was getting more familiar with the Bible since she had started to read it every morning. Brad's message about resting in the faithfulness of God spoke to her. She was gradually learning that Scripture wasn't rocket science, but was heart science, and if she listened with her heart, it would made perfect sense.

Lizzy locked the door after the last person had walked out, then jumped into Brad's car. "I know I am not virtuous, so tell me where we are going."

"Ha-ha. Lizzy, you are funny. Okay. We are going to the Duquesne Incline up to Mount Washington. There's a street art show going on today. We can mill about, and then I made early dinner reservations at Altius, an upscale restaurant overlooking downtown Pittsburgh."

"Very impressive, Brad. I haven't gone up the incline since probably the same time I went to a baseball game—twenty years ago. Sounds great."

They drove down Carson Street, which officially was considered the South Hills of Pittsburgh, then parked across the street and walked across to the entrance of the incline, and paid five dollars each for a round trip. The man handed them a brochure about the incline and a map of Grandview Avenue to look at once they got to the top.

Lizzy and Brad were the only people in the abbreviated wooden caboose-looking car, and they sat down on a wooden bench. Lizzy started to read the brochure. "'The incline was designed by Samuel Diescher and completed in eighteen-seventy-seven. It is eight hundred feet long, four hundred feet in height, and is inclined at a thirty-degree angle. It was originally used to carry cargo up and down Mount Washington and was steam-powered. It later became a means for people to go down to the city without walking on the connecting footpaths. It closed in nineteen -sixty-two for a total restoration, funded by local residents of the Duquesne Heights neighborhood. It reopened in 1963.'"

When Lizzy looked up from reading the brochure, the sight took her breath away. They were almost to the top when she noticed they were ascending over the treetops. The city across the river had become smaller, and she could see all the surrounding areas better, including the Fort Duquesne Bridge, which had suddenly become much smaller in size.

Brad and Lizzy exited the car and stepped onto a landing. The building had another entrance for the car that went down the mountain, as well as a gift shop. There was a machine that pressed a penny into a picture of the incline, and they decided that would make a great souvenir.

They went out of the building into a festive atmosphere on Grandview Avenue, made up of tents where people were walking around looking at the art and crafts. They turned right, and there, perched over the edge, was a lookout spot. They were both taken aback by the beauty. They could see the three rivers that met at the point where Fort Duquesne was located. It said on the sign it was called the "Golden Triangle." They truly could see for miles, and they stood in silence for a long time—with Brad's arm around Lizzy—until their senses could take no more. They rejoined the crowd out on the street to look at the art.

Brad and Lizzy arrived for their five o'clock reservation and walked into Altius. It, too, was perched over the hillside, surrounded by glass windows, and had a dynamic view of the city. They were seated by the windows.

"How did you get this table? Do you know someone?"

Brad chuckled and said, "No, I just used one of my other titles: Doctor. They didn't ask, so I didn't say 'doctor of theology.' I don't normally title drop, but I wanted this to be extra-special, like you. I also ordered in advance Chateaubriand for Two."

"What is that? French?"

"Yes, you will have to be virtuous and wait until it comes to see for yourself." They both laughed but not so loud, so as not to disturb the atmosphere.

The meal arrived just as the sun was going down. It was the most exquisite plate of sliced grilled tenderloin, surrounded by a ring of sculptured mashed potatoes that had been browned and covered in Béarnaise sauce. While they were eating, the lights of the downtown buildings came on, including PPG, USX, and the surrounding skyscrapers, and the fountains at the point lit up in different colors. Brad and Lizzy couldn't imagine anything more grand than Grandview Avenue, and they decided they would have to return when family—more specifically, Vickie and her family—came to visit, "if" they ever did.

Brad wanted to know what happened to her and her sister. He could tell that something was wrong between them. She didn't want to say that she was jealous, but she used the five-year difference in age as an excuse. Then, Lizzy changed her mind and told Brad the truth, that she was jealous of her sister, but likewise she felt like her sister had abandoned her. Although Brad had been an only child, he understood and appreciated that Lizzy trusted him enough to tell him the truth. It made him feel more connected with her. He felt sad for Lizzy and her sister, and he wished he could do something to get the two of them back on track.

CHAPTER 15

Lizzy was feeling sleep-deprived. If it hadn't been for Brad, she probably would have thrown in the towel by now. She now knew what "burning the candle at both ends" meant, and she was sure she could be the poster person for it. But one thing Lizzy knew was that she wasn't a quitter. Her mom and dad had instilled that in her. They would always quote those silly clichés: "When the going gets tough, the tough get going"; "what doesn't kill you makes you stronger"; "it will all be good at the end; if it's not good, it's not the end"; and the list went on. Lizzy thought maybe they kept a book of clichés in their back pockets, just in case. Lizzy wondered what her mom and dad would have said today if they were still alive, but she couldn't imagine there would a cliché good enough to make her want to continue running the pub.

She read her Bible and prayed, as she did every morning. She felt peace when she knew that God was working behind the scenes, that He was always working for His loved ones, like her. This energized her. She realized that God was the ultimate author of all clichés known to man, anyway. She surrendered it all to Him, and suddenly she felt invincible, ready to tackle the day. She finished her paperwork and found herself ready for whatever the day threw her way.

Cindy showed up at eleven. Lizzy and Cindy had become the best of friends. Lizzy would tell her about her dates with Brad and how deep her feelings were becoming. They talked about their childhoods, as they realized they were at different spectrums as far as their religious upbringings were concerned. But they both agreed that it wasn't how you got to God as long as you did get there. Cindy had become Lizzy's mentor, which in her mind, was the best gift of all. She still loved Bonnie, but Cindy could answer all of the questions about Jesus she would formulate every morning.

Lizzy was on her way to the bank when her cell phone rang. It was Brad.

"Hi, Lizzy. I am sorry, I can't come over for dinner tonight. I ran across some electrical issues at the church, and the electricians agreed to put me on their schedule for the end of the day. I was really looking forward to seeing you."

"That's not a problem, Brad. Electricity is something you don't fool around with. You certainly don't need an-

other fire. I will send David over with a to-go container
and to pick up the boys."

"You are the best. Thank you so much for understanding. I will definitely be there tomorrow night for
my favorite meat loaf. I love you and will call you later."

"Okie-dokie. Love you, too. Bye."

Lizzy hung up the phone and wrote on the erase
board: "Spaghetti with meatballs, zucchini, and bread."
She was ready to go. Suzie Q was working six days a
week now, because Lizzy needed to be the cook. CJ, who
had been faithfully at work by six, had been a lifesaver
by busing tables and washing dishes. Lizzy had given
both Suzie Q and CJ significant raises and put Crystal
and Maggie on the payroll. She didn't need to hire anyone else now, because her girls were very proficient at
waitressing and would help in other areas if needed.
Except for a few minor bumps, the pub was now running like a well-oiled machine.

A new face came in and sat down at the bar. Lizzy
heard him say his name was Jerry. Through his conversation, she learned he had just lost his job at Dailys for
something he didn't think he did, and that he was going
to hire an attorney for wrongful termination. He was
a big, burly guy, with a full beard and mustache. She
couldn't help noticing that, because he was ordering
a boilermaker—which was a shot of whiskey dropped

into a beer before the patron chugged it down. It put out a lot of foam, which was sticking to his beard.

"Suzie, can you come into the kitchen for a minute? There's something I want to show you."

"Sure, I will be right there." Suzie walked back to the kitchen. "What's up?"

"Try to get that guy to eat something, and try to get him to slow down on the drinks. He's already in a bad mood, and you know how that may go."

"Sure, I will keep an eye on him. And CJ will be here soon."

Suzie Q kept asking the guy if he wanted something to eat. He was starting to become belligerent and began demanding more alcohol. Just then Teddy Summer walked in. In a slurred voice, Jerry said, "What are you looking at, jerk?"

Teddy thought Jerry was being funny, and he said, "I have a mirror in front of my face. You're looking at yourself."

Jerry got up out of his chair, knocking the bar stool to the ground, and went after Teddy. He was just about to hit him when CJ walked in and stopped his blow in midair. He grabbed the guy by his shirt and belt and tossed him out the door onto the parking lot.

"If you know what is good for you, you will get out of here and go home. This is a respectable establishment, and you are permanently banned from ever coming back."

The man got off the ground and stumbled out of the parking lot and out of sight. CJ went back inside. "I don't think he will be back," he said. Famous last words, as a brick came crashing through the entry door, glass shattering everywhere. CJ ran out, but only saw taillights driving off in the distance.

Lizzy called the police and explained they had the man's first name but had no idea who he was or where he lived. The cops took notes about his description and were going to check at Daily's tomorrow to see who they had fired that day. The police officer said they would be in touch if they could locate the suspect.

Lizzy was shaking like a leaf. She was trying to figure out what hardware store was open for either plywood or two-by-fours to cover the hole in the door until morning, when she could call a glass company to put new glass in. Just then her cell phone rang. It was Brad.

"Oh, Brad, you won't believe what just happened." Lizzy sounded frantic.

She explained the incident to him. He told her that there was leftover wood at the church, and that he would be right there with the wood, hammer, and nails to secure it until she could get it fixed.

Brad was there in less than five minutes. He gave a big hug and told her it would be okay.

"I may be okay this time, but what about the next? What happens if next time some maniac comes back with a gun and someone gets hurt? I would feel so guilty. This would have never happened when my mom and dad ran the pub. What is wrong with people today?" Lizzy started to cry.

Brad comforted her. "You can't live on what-ifs—that's what Satan wants you to do. The guy is going to wake up with a hangover and hopefully feel remorse. It sounds like the cops will track him down by his looks and with the aid of the people at Dailys."

"I am sorry. I know I am overreacting, but I am tired. I'm tired of this place, too."

"I know, sweetheart, but it will be okay. I can sleep on your couch if that would make you feel safer."

"Thanks. I have an alarm system. I should be fine."

"Come on, Lizzy, let me protect you. Not because I have to, but because I want to."

She agreed and continued to clean up the mess. She was sure she had lost some business that night, because no one wants to go into a place where there are police cars with flashing lights. She decided to close at ten instead of midnight and told everyone they would get paid as though they had worked until midnight. Everyone hugged and kissed cheeks before they left, telling Lizzy to hang in there.

Brad slept on the couch while Lizzy slept like a baby, feeling protected.

CHAPTER 16

Lizzy woke up feeling refreshed and relaxed. She could smell the coffee, expecting to see Brad, but instead there was a note on the counter next to the pot of coffee. It said:

"Good morning, Sunshine, sorry I had to leave early. I received a text from the electrician that they are coming to the church at 7 a.m. I didn't want to tell you last night, but the wiring was severely defective. The electrician said he was surprised there hadn't been an electrical fire. They need to rewire the whole building.

"I hope you are feeling better. I have an analogy that I often use. Think of yourself on a bicycle built for two. You are in the back, and God is in the front steering. You will need to do your job and pedal, but the Creator of the universe will steer you in the right direction, so don't worry.

"I will call you later.

"Love,

Brad."

Lizzy felt better, knowing she had someone like Brad in her life. She just wished she weren't so skeptical. She thought, "I must let go and let God take over the steering." She felt some of the burden released as she sat down to read her Bible.

Brad called her while she was in the pub making meat loaf for later. "Are you feeling better now?"

"Yes, I feel a lot better. Thanks for the sweet note. How are you doing, and how's the wiring going?"

"It's going great. They said they will be done this afternoon. It's amazing to see how they can snake the wires through the walls. Of course, it's too bad that I didn't discover the problem while the drywall was down, but electricity is not my thing. What are you doing?"

"I am preparing your favorite meal."

"Meat loaf. Yummy. I can't wait. I know we made Sunday our date day, but I was wondering if you would like to go down to the National Aviary and eat at a German restaurant called Max's Allegheny Tavern on Wednesday. I don't know if I told you that I am German." He chuckled.

Lizzy gave a hearty laugh. "I would have never guessed, with the last name of Schmidt. Yes, I would really like that. It might be just what the doctor ordered, even if it's a doctor of theology."

"Great. But you are still in charge of Sunday's date."

Brad arrived at the pub at five o'clock to eat dinner, and he noticed the place was almost empty. He couldn't help thinking it was a result of last night's incident. The police had a suspect in mind, but they couldn't locate him and felt he had left the area. The good thing about that was that Lizzy could join him to eat.

"How did the wiring go?"

"All done. Thankfully the Landrys donated that money, because it just covered the repairs."

"How are you doing?"

"I am better. Thanks again for the analogy about the bicycle built for two. I really like that. I noticed Jesus used parables in His day, and they make it easier to understand. I guess twelve years of this was festering, and I didn't know I had become a walking pressure cooker."

"I know, Lizzy. I totally understand the pressure, because I feel it sometimes too. Those are the days when I get on the back of the bike."

"Yes, I think I understand, but it's so new to me not to be in control."

"'Control' sometimes can be an oxymoron. That's where the Serenity Prayer comes in."

"What is that?"

"The Serenity Prayer says, 'God, grant me the serenity to accept the things I cannot change; the courage to change the things I can; and the wisdom to know the difference.'"

"Wow, that's great. I am going to try to put those words into practice."

"Can I come get you at ten thirty tomorrow? I thought we'd go eat first, the restaurant opens at eleven, that way we might beat the large lunch crowd. Then we can walk off the calories at the Aviary."

"Sounds like a great escape."

"The great thing about this escape is that I get to do it with you. See you tomorrow." Brad kissed Lizzy and walked out of the pub.

The next day was a record high for that day, and hope was in the air that a much-anticipated spring was just around the corner. Brad and Lizzy made their way to the north side of Pittsburgh. Brad hadn't been there for a long time, and he drove around the Mexican War Streets for a short while.

Lizzy commented on how beautiful the attached row homes were. Brad explained what he remembered, that in the 1840s, they developed the land called Buena Vista. The streets were named after names and places from the Mexican-American War. He told Lizzy he had been in one of the homes that had been refurbished, and it was a beautiful three-story home. "The nice thing about it is that you can walk to downtown from here."

Brad and Lizzy finally found the restaurant. Max's was a quaint place with a lot of dark wood throughout. It had two connecting rooms filled with tables with floral tablecloths. The smells were overloading their appetite senses as the hostess walked them to their table next to the window, which ironically overlooked St. Peter's Parish, with a beautiful statue of Mother Mary across the street.

"Lizzy, you look so pretty in the sunlight. Do you want me to order the food?"

"Thank you. You look very handsome in the sunlight, too, and yes, you can order. I trust you, since the food is right up your German alley."

The waiter came to their table with a pad and paper in hand. Brad ordered two Sprites, two Einlauf soups, two Max's Famous Reubens, one hot German potato salad, and two potato pancakes.

"Wow, Brad, you must be hungry."

Brad laughed. "Didn't I tell you that I am a foodie?"

Lizzy giggled in return. "Another thing we have in common." Then she asked, "Where in Germany did your people come from?"

"My people came here in the early 1900s from Russia. They had migrated there from Germany, earlier to the southern region, then called Prussia, when they were giving Germany's land to farm. My great-grandmother Levi, whose husband had died during the Lenin Revolution, fled with my grandmother Rosina to the United States, right here to Pittsburgh. Rosina married my grandfather, Alfred Schmidt, and they relocated to

Verona to pastor the Lutheran church, and you know the rest."

Lizzy commented, "Levi sounds Jewish to me, are you?

"I supposedly am partially, but it was taboo to talk about it. I am not sure why, because the tribe of Levi were the priests and carriers of the Ark of the Covenant in the Old Testament. I think that sounds good to me. Perhaps one of these days I will take one of those ancestry tests, but to be honest, I just consider myself an American Christian."

They continued talking, and both agreed the food was delicious. Lizzy understood why it was a popular place. The hospital was just a few blocks away, so there were many people in scrubs and smocks. It got added to the list of places they wanted to return again later.

They made the short drive to the aviary. It was so unique to Lizzy to walk around birds that were not in cages. The crowned pigeons walked by their feet, and they hand-fed rainbow lorikeets and got up close to the salmon-colored flamingos. Lizzy couldn't believe all the different kinds of species: Besides the flamingos, there were penguins, eagles, parrots, and even a sloth.

As they were leaving the aviary, Brad asked, "So, what did you think about the aviary?"

"Are you kidding? I totally forgot I was in Pittsburgh. I absolutely had a blast today. Thanks. It's just what the very wise and astute doctor ordered."

Brad laughed out loud. "You are welcome. I am glad you enjoyed it. You deserve the best. I love you, sweetheart."

"I love you, too."

Lizzy got back after three o'clock, but she knew Susie Q could do her job probably better than even she could in opening up the pub. She felt refreshed, and she realized her life had become so different from others, because most people actually got out and explored as a normal part of their lives. She wondered what else she might have missed in her life before now, but she was thankful that at least her life was changing for the better. She was happy that she was able to share new places for the first time with Brad. She felt like it was much better exploring with another person, especially someone special like him.

CHAPTER 17

Lizzy was excited to go to church downstairs. If someone had asked her last month where she would be today, not in her wildest dreams would she have said this. Even the incident with the brick had seemed to evaporate to nothing. She was starting to feel so alive and full of hope. She thought, "I am the same old Lizzy, except so much better."

She had gotten up earlier to make sure her makeup and outfit were perfect. The outfit she was going to wear that day was the last of her new clothes. She liked the idea of going shopping again with Cindy to expand her wardrobe. She felt Cindy liked shopping as much as she did, and she really appreciated her sharing her fashion sense with her. She had even gone to Bonnie's salon on Friday. Bonnie had given her first real hairstyle, a modified bobbed haircut that just curved in at the ends. She had to admit to herself it looked pretty good on her.

Brad came into the Pub Pews Church and gave Lizzy a passionate kiss. "Hello, sunshine. You look beautiful as usual. There is something different—did you get a haircut?" He gave her a huge smile. "I can't wait to see what plans you have in store for our date today."

Lizzy was flattered that Brad had noticed her hair. "Do you want to know what we are doing?"

"Oh no, I don't want to give up my virtues. I can 'patiently' wait." He chuckled

"You're funny, Brad. Do you have a good sermon planned?"

"Yes, do you want to know about it?"

"Oh no, I don't want to give up my virtues either. I can 'patiently' wait." She chuckled in return.

Just then, the people started to arrive as more new faces were coming in. The word must have gotten out about the young, new dynamic preacher. Lizzy was so happy for Brad; he certainly deserved it. She counted 150 people. The service had always started with music. Three of the sweetest-looking girls, who looked to be about seven years old, in their even-sweeter pretty dresses, went up to the front and sang "Jesus Loves Me" in a capella. Lizzy couldn't imagine at any age getting up in front of anyone to sing or talk. She had a beautiful voice, but she was just too painfully shy to share it with anyone, especially a group of strangers.

After the girls finished their song, Brad told the congregation to turn to Matthew 6:26 in the New Testament. He read, "'Look at the birds of the air, for they neither sow nor reap nor gather into barns; yet your heavenly Father feeds them. Are you not of more value than them?' We are serving a God who loves us and wants to lavish His love on us. He loves us so much that He sent His only Son to atone for us. Jesus took our sins to the cross with Him, as it says in John 3:16: 'For God so loved the world that he gave his one and only son, that whoever believes in him shall not perish but have eternal life.'"

Brad went on with his sermon, telling them that God's love was unconditional and He wanted them to be His children. In return, He just wanted our love and respect. Lizzy loved the simplicity in the way Brad preached and how he always referenced the Bible.

After everyone walked out, Lizzy locked up, and they headed down to the south side part of Pittsburgh called Station Square, a beautiful, fifty-two-acre riverfront complex with over a mile of unique dining, entertainment, and boutique shopping. Lizzy had made a reservation at a restaurant called the Melting Pot, which specialized in fondues. They were lucky enough to get a window seat.

Lizzy asked, "You don't mind if I order for both of us, do you?"

"Not at all. I trust you completely, Lizzy."

She ordered a Wisconsin cheddar cheese fondue for two, followed by a flaming turtle dessert fondue, and two Sprites.

"Lizzy, that sounds great, especially the dessert."

"Should I call the waiter back and order the dessert first?"

Brad laughed. "You have such a great sense of humor. Did you get that from your mom or your dad?"

"My mom was the jokester in the family. I don't remember if I told you that she was British. That's how my sister and I got our names—after the queens, Victoria and Elizabeth. She was always laughing and joking. She would call herself the 'spunky, pleasantly plump woman from the Isles.' You would have liked her. I never met anyone who didn't have a kind word to say about 'me maw.' My dad was right on her heels as far as humor. He had an Irish sense of humor that was a wee bit more sarcastic but was equally as funny. We would say there was never a dull moment in our house. It was a loving, nurturing, fun home."

"I can see that about you, Lizzy. The apple and the tree are close."

"Thank you. We have reservations on the Gateway Clipper right out there on the water. I have lived on the river my whole life, but I have never been out in a boat on it."

"Me neither. I heard stories that the rivers would make you sick, back in the steel mill days, if you ingested any of it. I think they say the rivers are pretty clean now."

"Yes, I see lots of boats out my windows cruising up and down the river now. In fact, Pittsburgh has the second-largest registered pleasure boats in the country. There are seventeen marinas in Allegheny County along the three rivers."

"My, aren't you full of information." Brad chuckled.

"Yes, you tend to hear those things when you live on one of those rivers. We are going on a three-thirty, one-hour sightseeing tour called 'Pittsburgh: How It All Began.' It will share the importance Pittsburgh played in the French and Indian War, the Whiskey Rebellion, and the Civil War. We will learn about Pittsburgh's early days as a frontier village, how it became the Gateway to the West, and its history as a world leader in the production of glass, iron, and steel."

"How do you know all that?'"

"I read it on their web page." They both exploded in laughter.

The fondues were excellent. The other people in the Melting Pot no doubt could tell they were in love when they affectionately dipped the bread into the pot and fed each other, and then tenderly wiped their faces if they had gotten some of the cheese or chocolate on it. Brad and Lizzy were oblivious to everyone around them—the Queen of England could have been sitting next to them and they wouldn't have noticed.

After dinner, they walked down toward the river with their arms wrapped tightly around each other, then walked up a wooden plank to get on the Gateway Clipper. It was a colorful red, white, and blue river paddleboat with seating inside or up on the top deck. It was a beautiful day, so they opted to sit on top.

Brad and Lizzy enjoyed the scenery and the captain's history lesson as they paddled around all three of the rivers. They both agreed there was something mesmerizing and relaxing about being on the water. It was a whole new perspective seeing the city on the river.

It was another perfect day. Lizzy dropped Brad back at the church so that she could get back to clean and change the oil in the double fryer. They shared one more passionate kiss in the car, and as Lizzy drove off, Brad said to himself, "I am truly a blessed man. Thank You, God, for Lizzy."

CHAPTER 18

The next day, in lieu of the regular Sunday date, they were going on a group date on Thursday, April 2, to the Pittsburgh Pirates home opener against the Cincinnati Reds at 1:35 in the park downtown. Normally, the tickets would have been sold out, but Michael Landry had a friend who had a corporate box seat that wasn't going to be used because the company had a convention the same day. So, Michael and Cindy Landry, Bonnie Spencer, David Smith, and Brad and Lizzy headed downtown in Landry's car, all dressed up in gold and black.

Lizzy had gone to Dick's Sporting Goods by the mall by herself because Cindy had been busy that day. She bought herself a Roberto Clemente jersey, black sweats, and an Under Armor black turtleneck. Brad had an old Willie Stargell #8 jersey, and he wore black jeans. The others likewise wore some sort of Pirates attire. The men in the car were talking about Pete Rose and his chances of getting inducted into the Baseball Hall of

Fame. The three agreed that he would get inducted, but that it probably wasn't going to happen while he was still alive. The women were talking about more important things like fashion and hairstyles.

The streets were already a sea of black and gold. It was slow going down Broadway to the parking lot where Michael had gotten a pass from his friend. It was predetermined that they would be going to the Slice on Broadway restaurant that overlooked the Allegheny River across from downtown. When they arrived, there was a half-hour wait, so they decided to take a stroll along the walkway. Brad looked back at Lizzy while they were walking and couldn't get over how cute she looked in her Pirates wear. She reminded him of an enthusiastic cheerleader he had once known in school, she was so outgoing and liked by everyone.

No one noticed or cared, but the women and men had segregated from each other. It didn't matter, because everyone was having a great time. They watched as people crossed the Roberto Clemente Bridge, which was closed down to cars on game days. There were a few splashes of red color in the crowd, but mostly it looked like an army of black and gold.

The couples were reunited when they got back from the walk and sat down in the restaurant. After they ate, the couples held hands as they made their way to the stadium. They arrived at their box seats and walked in.

It was a two-tier room with a kitchen and bathrooms on the upper tier, with the lower tier facing the field with ample seating. The windows had the ability to be opened or closed.

"Wow, look at these seats!" David exclaimed. "I have never been to a game. My parents were too poor to take all of us kids. Now not only do I get to see a ballgame, but I get to see it in a first-class box seat. Thank You, Lord!"

Brad said, "Speaking of kids, I know Tony, Pete, and Kyle were disappointed that we wouldn't let them skip school to come, so why don't we go to the ticket window by the entrance and surprise them with weekend game tickets?"

David replied, "That's a great idea. Let's do that for sure."

"Lizzy, do you and Bonnie want to come too?"

Both women looked at each other and in unison said, "Why don't you make it a guys-only day?" They all agreed on that.

Even knowing they were full, they had to go get some peanuts and Cracker Jacks to bring the song, "Take Me Out to the Ballgame" to life in the seventh inning, keeping the tradition going. They all felt that being at the game was a much better experience in person. The energy of the crowd, the aromas of the food, the colors and the sounds, all were something you couldn't get by watching the game on TV. They all agreed that it had been a blast.

It was considerably quieter on the way home because they were all tired. The men did recap the part of the game where the Pirates won three to one, with vivid recollection of what player did what. The women sat in silence, asking in their minds, "Who cares?" In fact, it was making them more tired, hearing all those details, but they knew that was what males bonding would do.

Brad got out at the pub because he had a question to ask Lizzy. Michael was going to drop off David and Bonnie at Bonnie's house. Everyone said their good-byes.

Brad and Lizzy walked into the pub, where Suzie Q was talking to Teddy. Business had gone down after the brick incident, and it didn't look like it was going to rebound anytime soon, because the place was empty. Brad and Lizzy grabbed Sprites from the top of the bar and went and sat next to the sliders.

"I have a few questions for you, Lizzy. First, will you hand out the palm tree crosses this Sunday? It's Palm Sunday, and I always order them. All you need to do is stand by the door as the people come in."

"Sure, I would be happy to do that," she said.

"Secondly, I thought in lieu of going on a date on Easter Sunday, we could instead volunteer at the Salvation Army to serve the meals. They have an Easter egg hunt afterward and need help with that, too. My buddy,

Major Mark Sedacca, said they have a shortage of volunteers this year."

"Sure, to that too. It sounds great."

"Thanks for your understanding and for being so sweet about it. I will make the date up to you."

"Don't be silly. Just spending time with you is enough for me."

"You're the best, Lizzy. I love you."

"I love you, too. I am still in charge of this weekend. Have you ever been whitewater rafting?"

"No, but I have always wanted to."

CHAPTER 19

Lizzy stood at the garage door and handed out cross-shaped palm leaves to everyone who came through the door. Brad noticed that when the people came through the door, they responded positively toward Lizzy's bubbly personality and warm smile. She enthusiastically greeted them in a way that, Brad took note of, would make a perfect pastor's wife. He knew they hadn't been dating long, but they were both in their thirties, and he thought he would broach the subject on the way to whitewater rafting. He had no doubt in his own mind, but he wasn't a hundred percent sure about what Lizzy had in her mind. And they had never discussed children either. He had done premarital counseling with couples before, and that was one of those make-or-break subjects.

A young man sitting in front with his guitar began to sing Chris Tomlin's "Our God." Lizzy thought it was a nice upbeat song.

Brad stepped up to the pulpit and told everyone to open their bibles to Romans 8:31–32: "'What shall we say about such wonderful things as these? If God is for us, who can ever be against us? Since he did not spare even his own Son but gave him up for all, won't he also give us everything else?'"

Lizzy was understanding the words better. Brad wasn't saying that they wouldn't have people or circumstances come against them, but that God would stand with them and no one could take on the Creator who lived in their heart, even death could not part them.

Lizzy now sat in front because it was closer to the door. This week she couldn't count how many people attended the service, but she felt like the number had increased.

When Brad shook the last hand, he turned to Lizzy. "Are you ready for some fun? Did you pack some extra clothes? We are going on the intermediate part of the whitewater at Ohiopyle, but I think we may still get wet. I will go down and change and pick you up in fifteen minutes. We are going to make a quick stop at Frank Lloyd Wright's Fallingwater. It's on the way. There is an hourlong tour of the home, and I booked us for the last trip down the rapids. I got some subs and drinks from the grocery to take with us."

"You're wonderfully organized, another thing we have in common," Lizzy said with a big grin. "I will be out front in fifteen."

Brad and Lizzy headed down the turnpike. It would take an hour and fifteen minutes to get to Frank Lloyd's Wright's Fallingwaters, and Brad wanted to have a heart-to-heart talk on the way. The conversation started out light, with Lizzy asking Brad some additional information about his sermon. That was easy for him. He felt like he had swallowed a pinecone, because he had a nervous feeling in his stomach. He felt confident, but what if he was missing Lizzy's signals? "Lord, help me to use the right words," he was praying in his head.

"Lizzy, what are your views about marriage and babies?"

"Well, I think you should get married before you have babies." She chuckled.

"Seriously, what do you think?"

Lizzy could immediately tell this wasn't a time to be funny. "Marriage to me has seemed like a faraway land, and I didn't have a way to get there. Do I want to get married? Absolutely! Of course, it would have to be a special kind of guy, a guy who is sweet, considerate, respectful, and fun... Exactly someone like you, and yes, I want kids—the more the merrier."

"Those are the exact words I wanted to hear come out of your mouth. So, how long do we wait?"

"Well, let's face it. We are no longer a spring chicken and a young rooster. I think there are no guarantees. Look at my mom and dad both dying so young. If we are going to let fear rule the roost, we might never get out of the chicken coop."

Brad exploded with laughter. "That analogy is spot-on. I love how your brain works, and I love you."

The ride was pleasant now that all the guesswork was over about how they felt about each other. They both realized that they wanted the same thing—which was each other.

When they got to Fallingwater, they had a few minutes before the tour began. Brad handed the women the tickets that he had downloaded to his phone. There were only ten people total, but there were many tours going simultaneously.

The tour guide started, "Fallingwater is a house designed by architect Frank Lloyd Wright in 1935. The house was built partly over a waterfall on Bear Run, located in the Laurel Highlands of the Allegheny Mountains. The house was designed as a weekend home for the Kauffmans, owners of Kauffman's department store. The house was designated a National Landmark in 1966, and it has had over five million people visit it since then." She continued with a lot more facts as they toured the property. Lizzy and Brad were mesmerized by its unusual beauty and the architectural design located in beautiful, unspoiled surroundings.

"Lizzy, can you imagine coming up with a house designed like this?"

"No. Frank Lloyd Wright definitely thought outside the box as far as architecture. I think he must have had such a creative, God-given mind. This is such an awesome home. I am so glad that you brought me here. I am not so sure I would have picked it. It must mean you have a creative, God-given mind, too. Thanks, darling, for opening my eyes to a whole new world, both in the flesh and in the spirit."

Brad was so touched by the words. He gave Lizzy a heartfelt kiss and a drawn-out bear hug.

They totally enjoyed the tour, saying they definitely wanted to come back again someday. Then they got into Brad's car and headed to Ohiopyle, which was about twenty minutes away.

When they pulled up, there was a diverse population of all ages, colors, and body types. Lizzy was amazed by how busy it was. The parking lot was full, and there were happy people chatting everywhere.

After Brad and Lizzy parked, they went up to the ticket window. "Hi, my name is Brad Schmidt. I have reservations for the intermediate express trip." The other trips furnished food. But they had eaten the food Brad brought with them on the way there. The express without food took two to three hours, compared to the other one where they stopped to eat, which took three to five hours. After they ran Brad's credit card. they handed him a brochure on the procedures, precautions, and recommendations for their trip. They both had to sign a waiver form as well. They were told to meet their expert guides, Bill Aubuchon and his wife, Belinda, at dock number three. There would be another couple joining them for their ultimate whitewater rafting experience.

The Aubuchons were the epitome of an all-American athletic couple. They were both warm and friendly. Brad and Lizzy felt confident about their abilities to get them down the III- and IV-rated rapids safely. The other couple was also athletic, a black couple who were really friendly, down to earth, and excited about the experience. Their names were Jim and Gloria Matthews.

Brad asked Jim and Gloria if they had ever done this before and they said, "No, this is our first time, and you?"

"It's a first for us as well. I have to admit, my heart is racing like the sound of that thunderous, raging water."

Bill said, "This is the best time of year, with the snowmelt and rain. The rapids on the upper Youghiogheny River are the fastest. I promise you that you're going to have the time of your lives. The river is at its peak this year, so it's a continuing adventure with very few breaks in between. I hope you had your Wheaties this morning, and your arms are healthy."

"Sounds great. No one has gotten hurt doing this, right?" Jim Matthews asked.

"Not on the intermediate, and never with the professional rafting guides. Belinda and I started rafting when we were in our teens, over twenty years ago, so you don't need to worry. We know these rapids like the backs of our hands."

Lizzy's stomach went halfway up to her throat, because she had never told Brad that she couldn't swim. She didn't want to appear to be flawed, saying to herself, "That's what the lifejacket is for. So, just relax and have fun. Yikes." Her thoughts and stomach were in freefall now. "Take some deep breaths before you pass out," she said in her head.

"Lizzy, you look apprehensive. Actually, you look downright frightened."

"I didn't want to tell you this, but I don't know how to swim."

Brad chuckled and gave Lizzy a hug. "When my grandfather joined the navy, he didn't know how to swim either."

"Was your grandfather always afraid?"

"No, he trusted God, but that's also why he ordered my dad and me to learn how to swim. Lizzy, you will be fine. I will save you if you fall in. And I will teach you how to swim this summer."

"Thanks. You are my aqua-prince." They both laughed out loud.

The women sat in front of the raft, the men in the middle of the raft, and the guides, Bill and Belinda, manning the rudders. Lizzy was sure that she and Gloria absorbed most of the white water spray and that they had acted as shields for the men.

Regardless, Lizzy and Gloria would look at each other after a stretch of rapids and give each other a high-five to indicate that they survived. She turned to Brad and gave him two thumbs up. By the end of the white water tour, a bond had been created between both couples as an accomplishment that they had all defeated the rapids and were still there to talk about it.

They definitely were wise to bring extra clothes because they had gotten soaked to the bone with extremely cold water. All four of them—Jim, Gloria, Brad, and Lizzy—had now bonded by living through this experience. They exchanged telephone numbers and found out that the Matthews lived in the North Hills called Treesdale, an Arnold Palmer golf community, not too far from each other. They tentatively set up a date in May to meet for dinner.

The ride home was quiet. Lizzy and Brad's arms hadn't seen that much action in a long time. Lizzy finally warmed up halfway home and fell sound asleep. Brad looked over at her sleeping. "Thank You, God, for sending me this angel."

Later, he said, "I hate to wake you up, Lizzy, but we are home." She woke up with a jerk, forgetting where she was.

Then, sleepily, she said, "Good night. Thanks. I love you," and she turned to walk up the stairs.

"Good night, sweetheart. I will call you in the morning, but not too early."

CHAPTER 20

Lizzy was sore all over from the white water rafting trip. She was feeling good about her relationship, but she felt the total opposite about the pub's business, especially as she was adding up the receipts from Saturday. The bottom line was the same as before the fire at the church. She would have to let go of Crystal and Maggie as waitresses, but she figured they would not mind because their tips were diminished, and she would have to go back to working on Mondays. She started to wonder if she was doing something wrong in her spiritual life and if God was mad at her. She would have to put those thoughts on the back burner because she had a lot to do before Cindy got there to prepare the pasta dishes.

Just then her phone rang. "Hello?"

"Hi, Lizzy, this is Cindy. I am not going to be coming today. I just took inventory and we have enough Italian food for this week."

"That's okay. I still need to clean and change the oil in the deep fryer, and to make things worse, I have the smallest bank deposit I've had in a while. I feel like God is punishing me for something, but I'm not sure what."

"That's just Satan whispering lies into your ears. Have faith. It will be okay. How was your date yesterday?"

"It was fabulous, and that's what I'm hanging on to. We even had a discussion about marriage and children. I don't know why he would want me with this pub ball and chain around my neck."

"Lizzy, take a little break and pray. It always helps me, and things change for the best."

"I will, Cindy. Thank you for being such a dear friend. I will call you later. Thanks for calling me and letting me know about today."

Lizzy got off the phone and said, "Great, there goes more money out the window." But then she began to pray, and suddenly there was that indescribable peace. Somehow she knew it was going to be alright.

Lizzy went through her list. She had made marinara sauce over rigatoni and decided that she might as well do the meat loaf at the same time. She called Suzie Q and told her that she didn't need to come in tonight and she could stay home and watch Dancing with the Stars with her family.

Just then, her cell phone rang again. "Hello, sunshine. How's it going?"

Lizzy tried to sound positive, but apparently it didn't work.

"You sound upset. Is everything okay?"

"Yes, except there's no business, Cindy just cancelled, and it's just frustrating, that's all. I will get over it."

"Well, you are going to have one customer—me. I will be over at six to eat. Don't forget the boys: Tony, Pete, and Kyle, Bonnie, David, the Summer brothers plus one, and the three musketeers."

"The three amigos!" She chuckled while correcting him. He had a way of making her happy.

"Try not to worry that pretty little face of yours. I will see you later. Until then, hang in there."

"Okay, thanks for the pep talk. Love you."

"Love you, too."

Lizzy finished her setup for opening the pub, grabbed the cash register drawer, and then unlocked the door.

Bonnie and David came in after they dropped the boys at the church. Bonnie told her, "They are getting close to the end of painting the interior. They just have the entry and bathrooms left to do. Brad made mention that maybe they could paint the outside during the summer months and actually get paid. The boys were all excited about that prospect. They did a great job, and I was surprised how they took such pride in doing a good job. I think it was a real boost for their self-esteem. They even joked about starting a painting company after they graduate. Those boys are the proof of the power of prayers and the Lord."

That news made Lizzy happy, and besides that, Teddy, Ken, his wife, Irene, and the Daily amigos hadn't abandoned the pub yet. If she could get to May, the summer crowd would be back, and she would have a fighting chance to stay in business.

Brad, David, Bonnie, Tony, Kyle, and Pete all sat down and ate Lizzy's delicious spaghetti dinner. Lizzy actually had a chance to sit for a few minutes because there wasn't anyone else in the pub. Brad couldn't help but notice that Lizzy looked tired and sad. If he could only figure out a way for her to get out from under the weight of the pub, he would do it in a heartbeat.

The week was uneventful for Lizzy. She got caught up on tedious little jobs like soaking all the fountains and tap heads, cleaning in the corners, and wiping down the bottles and shelves. She cleaned all the refrigerators out and emptied the ice machine to restart a fresh batch of ice. She was trying to keep busy and remember what she had and not dwell on the things she didn't.

Brad had been working on his Easter service, and he reminded Lizzy that they were going to the Salvation Army to feed the hungry and help the little ones in their Easter egg hunt. Lizzy thought that would be something new to look forward to.

Easter Sunday was cooler than most Easters in the past. It was gray, and snow was imminent. Brad thought that the children were going to either bundle up or the Easter Bunny was going to have to drop his eggs inside.

Brad came into the pub and gave Lizzy a big kiss. "Are you ready to put on the bunny suit?"

Lizzy's eyes became as big as Frisbees. "What? You never said anything about a bunny suit."

"Gotcha, Lizzy Murphy. Just kidding with you."

"You are starting to remind me of my dad, who was the king of pranks. So, you, Brad Schmidt, had better beware, because I learned from the best." She giggled.

"Let me get ready for the sermon today. Easter is my favorite, because if it wasn't for the cross and the empty tomb, we wouldn't have a chance to make it into God's kingdom. The Salvation Army is at the corner of Frankstown and Blackadore, and lunch starts at one o'clock, so we will have to hightail it out of here after we're done."

The people started filing in an orderly fashion. Everyone was dressed nicely in floral dresses, and most of the men had on jackets and ties.

A woman in her forties came to the front with a keyboard and sang the "Easter Song" by Nicole Mullen. Her voice was angelic, and her volume and range were superb. Lizzy thought she could have listened to that all day.

Brad encapsulated John 20 and emphasized the fact that we could go to all the gravesites of the prophets, like Buddha or Mohammed, and we would find human remains. But Jesus' tomb was empty, and His remains were not there, to prove to everyone that He was who He said He was, God in the flesh. Also, over five hundred people had seen Jesus' resurrected body when He came back for forty days after His crucifixion. Brad pointed out that the probabilities of that many people seeing Jesus were astronomical. Brad said a statistical large number, that all those people witnessed the exact same thing was impossible. Brad's point was that the cross where Jesus took our sins and paid the price that we might live in God's kingdom, and the empty tomb, prove that Jesus lives in spirit like we will, and that all we have to do is to turn away from our sinful nature, pick up the cross, and follow Him.

After the last person left the Pub Pews Church, Brad and Lizzy grabbed their coats and headed to the Salvation Army. Brad saw his buddy, Major Mark, and asked where they were needed. Mark gave them each a plastic apron, a hairnet, and plastic gloves. He walked them over to a long table that had large warmers filled with potatoes and gravy.

"Brad, you will scoop the potatoes, and Lizzy, you will ask each person if they want gravy and pour on as much as they want. We have plenty of gravy. Then, you will pass the plate down the line so Linda can put on a roll, and she will pass it to Lori to add a dessert. In other words, it's a food assembly line. After everyone goes through once, they can come back for seconds. We had over five hundred people last year, so that's why we have four lines this year. You are going to have to move fast, but don't forget your smile, because it might be the only smile they see all week."

After the food service was done, Brad and Lizzy were assigned to the gym to oversee the egg hunt for the children five years old and younger. It was crowded with little kids and their parents, who were trying to hold them back from running to pick up the colored plastic eggs scattered all over the gym floor. Lizzy noticed that even the kids seemed to be drawn to Brad. He had a natural way of engaging them in conversation, and at one point there were a half dozen little ones surrounding him, looking up at him, waiting for his next question toward them. Lizzy knew for sure he was going to be a great father. She had already established he was going to be a great husband.

Major Mark dropped a green flag to initiate the collection of the eggs. It seemed to Lizzy that the parents were doing all the collecting, but the kids seemed happy even if they only had one egg. There was one little boy who appeared to be handicapped; delayed in his pursuit of the eggs, he had an empty basket. Mark had that covered with an extra basket that was full and handed it to him.

Lizzy looked at some of the faces that seemed down and out, and she felt such compassion toward them. She thought she had been coming to bless them, but all she felt was blessed herself to be the hands and feet of Jesus to them. She was ashamed that she'd had a pity party earlier that week, and she made the promise that she would never take her blessings for granted again.

CHAPTER 21

As Brad and Lizzy were on their way back from the Salvation Army, they should have felt exhausted, but actually they felt quite energized from the day's events.

"So, what did you think about today, Lizzy?"

"I felt so moved by the church service, and I was surprised at how volunteering gave me a feeling that no amount of money could give. In fact, I talked to Major Mark, and he gave me the phone number of Captain Sharna, who coordinates the volunteers. He said they could use help in the kitchen, because the number of people who utilize the facility to eat has doubled in the last year."

"Yes, that's what he told me, too. They are now serving over six hundred meals a day to the two hundred residents who stay there and the homeless—or, as he called them, 'neighbors,' a name they were given to show them some respect."

"I sometimes think we forget how good we have it. Now that I am aware there is a problem, I decided I am going to volunteer at least once a week, or more if I can scrape out any extra time."

"That's great, Lizzy. I know you will be great at doing that because I know how you love to feed people. I believe Jesus would be happy, too, that you are feeding His people."

"Thank you. You are so sweet to say that."

"I thought I would help you clean when we get back to the pub. I will even volunteer to clean your deep fryer."

Lizzy chuckled. "You'd better swing by the church first and grab your painting clothes, because the grease won't come out in the wash."

They stopped by the church, which was scheduled to open in a few weeks. Lizzy thought that except for the bare floors, it looked like a new building, but she had nothing to compare it to because she had never seen the inside of it before the fire.

"This looks great. Are you happy with the results?"

"I suppose I should say that I wished it had never caught fire in the first place, but then I would have never brought the pews to your place, and I might never have met you. So, yes, I am very happy with the results."

Lizzy opened the door to the pub. "Let the games begin."

Brad laughed. "It can't be that bad. Can it?"

"I will let you decide."

Cleaning the deep fryer was pretty horrific, but Brad took the bad with the good. They decided as they cleaned the pub that since it was two weekends before the reopening of the church, they would go to the opening of the season of Kennywood on April twenty-fifth. After all, it was the last official day that the pub was still going to be a church. They wanted to do something that would be equally exciting.

That meant they had one more Sunday on the nineteenth, and Lizzy was in charge. She thought she had better put on her thinking cap or just ask Cindy for a suggestion on what to do. She was scheduled to come over the next day to prepare the Italian dishes, so she would ask her then.

Between the two of them, they had the pub, including the deep fryer, cleaned and ready for Monday's opening. Brad and Lizzy worked excellent together, in perfect harmony, with a playful and fun way of doing it.

Cindy came over Monday at eleven o'clock, her usual time. Lizzy was always happy to see her. They had talked so much in the last month, there wasn't any stone unturned and no hidden secrets that hadn't already been discussed. In Lizzy's mind, Cindy had filled the sister void left by Vickie. Cindy enjoyed the freshness of her new Christian friend. She remembered the enthusiasm she felt when she first became a Christian.

"I need your help, Cindy. It's my turn to pick for date night again, and I am clueless."

"Well, my friend, you are not going to believe this, but we were supposed to go to the Penguins playoff game with another couple on Sunday evening, and they just cancelled. Their daughter's baby came early, so they can't go with us now, because they are going to see the newest addition to their family."

"Oh, Cindy, you are not joking with me, right?"

"No, I am serious. We have their box seats. They just gave them to us."

"Thank You, Lord. That's so exciting. I am sure Brad will be thrilled. What time is the game?"

"The game starts at seven p.m. They are playing the Tampa Bay Lightning. It's supposed to be a good game."

"I have never been to a hockey game before—ever. I had better google 'hockey rules' to read how it is played so I can tell what is going on during the game. This means I need some Penguin attire. Great. I can pick some up at the Strip District on Friday. Maybe I should get a Steelers shirt while I am there, just in case." Lizzy laughed.

Lizzy and Cindy finished their preparation of zucchini lasagna and put the last tray into Cindy's car.

"I will call you on Friday to make sure that you and Brad are all set for the hockey game on Sunday. Try not to work too hard in between. Love you." Cindy called through the car window before she left.

Lizzy thought that was a great way to start the week. She was hoping the rest of the week would follow as well. She called Brad first thing to tell him about the hockey game. He, too, was excited. He told Lizzy that he had actually played hockey through middle school. There was a rink across the river in Harmarville, but he had had to quit when he tore his Achilles' tendon. He and his dad would go to the Penguins games once a year, but that would have been over twenty years ago.

"That's so great, Lizzy. I can't wait."

"Since you know about hockey, perhaps you can teach me the game because I have no idea about the sport, except when the three amigos scream at the big screen while watching a game."

"I will be glad to teach you. I thought at one point in my life I wanted to be a professional hockey player, but God had other plans for me. I am much happier about those plans." He looked affectionately into Lizzy's eyes.

The week flew by, until it reached Sunday. The air outside was chilly but not cold. Lizzy thought she would wear her dress today. She was growing more confident that she and Brad's relationship was solid. Business had rebounded a little since the brick-throwing incident, but at this point, she didn't care as much because she no longer was living for the pub but for Jesus instead.

Brad walked in, dressed in khaki pants, a plaid shirt, and a solid sweater vest. Lizzy couldn't believe that this gorgeous man was hers. They shared a passionate kiss, knowing that it would have to tide them over until they could be alone again. Sure enough, his congregation started to arrive. The young man with the guitar whose name was Joe set up his chair, mic, and amplifier up front. Lizzy took note as the people arrived. It seemed to her that the people always spoke in low, melodious voices as they came in. It was quite the contrast, she thought, to the sounds of her bar, which were loud and cantankerous in comparison.

Joe started the service by singing, "Light Shine Bright" by Toby Mac. Lizzy thought it was a happy, up-beat song and she caught herself tapping her foot.

Brad then got up and spoke a heartfelt prayer that moved Lizzy to the core.

"Turn to Matthew 5:16," then Brad started to read: "'In the same way, let your light shine before men, that they may see your good deeds and praise your Father in heaven.'"

Brad preached to the congregation about the Salvation Army and the many service groups where they could become the hands and feet of Jesus. He came to serve, not to be served, and His followers should do the same. Their goals should be to reflect well for the Lord. This light might start the non-believers to ask questions that open the doors for them to fulfill what Jesus commissioned them to do, to share the good news. Jesus was their light, and they were blessed to get to the truth. Shouldn't they want to take the people who were walking in the darkness of death into the light, where there would be an eternity of beautiful spiritual life in heaven?

Brad continues, "I know as Christians, we don't want to get into controversial subjects, but we should ask ourselves, 'Why not?' We are not a façade for hopelessness, but we are the only hope for those still left in the dark." With that, Brad finished with an invitation and a prayer to actively become the beacon God wanted them to be.

The Landrys, Brad, and Lizzy left early to grab a bite to eat before the hockey game. They collectively decided to go to a restaurant on Fifth Avenue near the hockey arena called Buford's Kitchen. It was a quaint, contemporary restaurant offering American pub fare. Everyone ordered something different from the menu, thinking it was a good idea to sample it all. Lizzy ordered the shrimp and grits: shrimp sautéed with Cajun butter sauce over cheese grits with a fried egg garnish. Brad ordered the spicy Mississippi chicken breast sautéed with house barbecue sauce and served with a vegetable medley and rice. Michael ordered the jambalaya: ham, andouille, shrimp, and chicken, cooked with tomatoes, peppers, onions, Cajun seasoning, and rice. Cindy decided on the fried smothered catfish with Cajun crawfish sauce over rice with a vegetable medley. The food was delicious. They even jokingly started to talk like they were from Louisiana.

They parked in a reserved spot outside the PPG Paints Hockey Arena and proceeded to their mid-ice box seats. Brad and Michael were talking about the past great players like Mario Lemieux and Jaromir Jagr, but they both agreed their favorite was Ron Francis, who brought two Stanley Cups home to Pittsburgh.

Cindy and Lizzy, on the other hand, talked about more important things like makeup, fashion, and recipes. They were, however, impressed at how fast the players could skate, like they were flying on air. They both agreed that it was amazing they could do that on blades of steel and thought the game was quite exciting.

At the end of the night, the couples agreed they needed to get together more often socially, because they really enjoyed each other's company tremendously.

CHAPTER 22

It was a beautiful, fresh spring-like day in Pittsburgh. Lizzy was one step beyond exhausted, and she wondered how she would feel in thirty years when she was sixty-one. She wiped those thoughts and the sleep out of her eyes and headed downstairs to do her Monday preparations before Cindy arrived. She went through a recap of the Penguin game in her mind. She had liked the fast pace of the game, but she was still confused why the crowd got so excited when the players fought each other. It reminded her of sharks during a feeding frenzy. Nevertheless, she told herself that she and Brad should go again, because she could see how happy it had made him.

Cindy showed up exactly at eleven. Lizzy gave her credit for her punctuality and was amazed at how Cindy never seemed stressed out about anything. She figured that must be from her faith and decided that she should strive to be more like her friend.

"Good morning, Cindy. How are you doing today?"

"Good morning. I feel sleep-deprived. I am used to going to bed early because I get up at four to start the breakfast routine for Casey's. I let one of my assistant managers take over this morning, but I still couldn't sleep past four. Do you have any coffee?"

"I am with you. Let me put an extra-strong pot on."

It wasn't long into their preparing the Italian dish when the phone rang in the pub. It startled Lizzy, because it so rarely rang.

"Hello. Allegheny River Pub, this is Lizzy speaking."

"Hello. Is this Lizzy Murphy?"

"Yes, it is."

"This is the Verona Police Department. My name is Officer Lange."

"What can I help you with, Officer Lange?"

"We believe we may have the person who vandalized your establishment with a brick. His name is Jerry Pratt. We want you to come down to the station and see if you can identify him in a lineup."

"I would be happy to do that. I will be there in five minutes."

Lizzy hung up the phone and told Cindy what was going on. Cindy insisted that she would be fine and could continue without her. Lizzy grabbed her purse and proceeded to the police station.

She went to the front desk and asked for Officer Lange. Officer Lange came out from the back. She was tall, athletic, and a pretty woman—not at all what Lizzy had thought she sounded like on the phone.

"Hello. Follow me. I am going to take you into a room with one-way glass. Then we are going to bring in six men, and if you recognize any of them, you will let us know. Do you understand?"

Lizzy's heart rate jumped up quickly. "Yes."

The officer led Lizzy down a long hall into a dark room. Lizzy could see through the glass a brightly lit room with six numbers high on the wall and six black circles on the floor below them. While she was waiting in the dark room, the wheels in her head were turning. She was becoming apprehensive—what if she couldn't remember? It had happened so fast, and it had been over a month since the incident. She certainly didn't want to accuse the wrong person. Then it hit her like a brick, and forgiveness came to her mind. Those weren't her thoughts, because she had wanted revenge for Jerry ruining her business and causing her a huge inconvenience, yet the word forgiveness stuck in her mind.

The men finally started to file in. They all were so similar in looks and stature, big and burly. Lizzy was amazed that the police could find six men that were that close in appearance. They all turned to face Lizzy. The men were asked individually to step forward by their numbers. Lizzy immediately thought that Jerry was number three, but she wasn't a hundred percent sure. She couldn't help noticing how he looked like his life was on the line. She suddenly felt the shift from anger to sorrow for the man.

After all six had taken their turn stepping forward, Officer Lange asked Lizzy if she could identify one of the men. Lizzy, caught in pure conflict, asked herself, "What would Jesus do?"

Lizzy answered. "No. I don't see that man in this lineup."

"Are you sure?"

"Yes. I am sure."

Lizzy wasn't sure at first that she should have done that, but in her heart she knew it was the right thing to do. She grabbed her purse and went back to the pub.

When she returned to the pub, she told Cindy the whole story. Cindy didn't even ask her if she thought that was the right thing to do, because she felt that she had consulted with the right person, Jesus, and she left it at that.

Cindy drove off while Lizzy had little doubt that letting the guy go was the right thing. She knew he had drunk too much that night, on top of getting fired. She knew that everybody did stupid things in their lives, and she didn't think that was enough for her to ruin his life. But most importantly, she believed that was what the Holy Spirit was telling her to do.

Lizzy finished writing the daily special on the board and unlocked the door. She had gone back to letting Suzie Q off on Mondays. She was just wiping down the counters behind the bar when Jerry Pratt walked through the door, but he was smiling this time.

"I know you gave me a second chance today. Here's a hundred-dollar bill, and if you let me know the total cost for the window, I would like to pay you back in full. I am also very curious why you didn't press charges against me."

"Well, Jerry, you can thank God for that. He sent His Son, Jesus, to die for us all. He atoned for our sins, then forgave us before He died on the cross. He loves you, too. That's why."

Jerry laid his head down on the bar and openly wept. "I am so sorry for my actions that night. There hasn't been a day that has gone by since then that I haven't felt guilty. How do I find this Jesus you are talking about?"

Lizzy was taken by surprise, but she knew the door was opened, and even in her inexperience she knew she must step through it. She managed to fumble through a prayer with Jerry of repentance and acceptance of Jesus, not really knowing where the unrehearsed words came from.

Jerry wept deep from his soul, but he felt like a new person at the end.

Lizzy gave him a soda and they talked. She told him about the church. He said without a shadow of doubt he would be there on Sunday. He told Lizzy that he had lined up a new job, and now that he wasn't going to have a police record, he was going to start tomorrow.

The first thing Lizzy did after Jerry left was to call Brad. She told him the whole story.

Brad himself was fighting back tears, but they were tears of happiness. "Lizzy, you have no idea how proud I am of you, and how much I truly love you. You have done what some more-seasoned Christians might have struggled to do. I am sure the heavens are rejoicing, too."

The rest of the day was euphoric for Lizzy. She told Carlos about what happened when he arrived at six, informing him that Jerry's ban from the pub had been expunged. The rest of the week went equally well.

CHAPTER 23

On Sunday morning, Lizzy jumped out of bed, excited about church, seeing Brad preach, and going to Kennywood. She had heard so many stories over the years from other people who had told her their stories about Kennywood. She had always wanted to go, but now that the day had come, it seemed to take a back burner to her excitement about going to church.

The weather was perfect, expected to top out at seventy degrees later that day. Lizzy had dressed casually because she was going to keep the same outfit on to go to Kennywood. Brad arrived at ten thirty, wearing a pink polo shirt and gray pants.

"Good morning, sunshine. It looks like the weather is going to be perfect to go to Kennywood today."

"Good morning. I saw the weather is going to be outstanding. You must have some great connections." Lizzy giggled.

They shared a long kiss and a hug before Brad headed to the pulpit with his notes.

Joe came in, this time with his friend Steve, and set up two chairs. Steve had a banjo, and Joe had a guitar. After they got the mics in place, they waited for their cue from Brad.

After everyone had made their way to their seats and gotten settled, Brad nodded at Joe and Steve.

Joe announced that the name of the song was "Cast the First Stone" by Bradley Walker. It was an upbeat duet ballad about Jesus' encounter with an adulterous woman. Lizzy liked the banjo sound that she had never heard before, and she liked that it told a story through a song.

Brad started with a prayer and then told the congregation to turn to John 8. He started to tell the story of Jesus going to the temple at the Mount of Olives to teach the people there. The Pharisees were trying to trap Jesus and brought to Him a woman who had been caught in adultery. Then, the Pharisees said that by Moses' law, she must be stoned to death. Jesus instead bent down and wrote on the ground, then said, " If anyone of you is without sin, let him be the first to throw a stone."

All the Pharisees started to leave until only Jesus was left, and then He asked the woman, "Woman, where are they? Has no one condemned you? No one, sir, she said. Then neither do I condemn you, Jesus declared. Go now and leave your life of sin."

This message hit Lizzy right in her heart. It was what she had experienced with Jerry earlier in the week. Jerry had felt it, too, and he was the first person at the altar to make public his profession of faith. Lizzy was starting to see for herself God's loving hands. He was in control. How could something so simple yet so extraordinarily awesome have been there the whole time? She was beyond thankful. She thought to herself that no one should throw stones because they might come back and hit them in the face. No one had the right to judge anyone else, except Jesus, our sin-free Lord.

Brad looked at Lizzy after they locked up the pub and got into his car. "Are you ready for a day of rides, laughs, and signature food at Kennywood?"

"You sound like an advertisement for the park."

"Well, that's what I read on their webpage." They both broke out in laughter.

"Here. I printed out a map and descriptions of the rides and food. They also have fireworks right before they close at ten o'clock."

Lizzy loved the way Brad had taken the extra time to plan the day. The details that she read helped her decide on what rides they should go on, what to eat, and what she wanted to see. She felt confident that Brad was going to be in agreement with her. They hadn't disagreed on anything so far, an affirmation they were meant to be together.

Lizzy read out loud the information that was on the sheet. "'Founded in 1898, Kennywood has thrilled and delighted both young and young-at-heart for more than one hundred and twenty years.' I think we would be considered the young-at-heart." She laughed out loud.

"'Founded as a recreational playground far away from the bustle of downtown, the idyllic site overlooks the Monongahela River. It was designated a National Historic Landmark in 1987, and you'll find three roller coasters that date back to the 1920s, each as fun as the day they opened a century ago.' Wow! Those are some old roller coasters. We definitely have to ride them."

Lizzy took a pen and circled the rides that she was interested in. "Here are the rides that sounded good to me: Aero 360, Steel Curtain, Black Widow, Phantom's Revenge, Noah's Ark, the Exterminator, Jack Rabbit, Racer, Sky Rocket, Thunderbolt, Pirate, Turtle, and the paddle boats."

Brad laughed out loud. "Did you leave anything out? Lizzy Murphy, I think you are going to wear me out even before we get there."

They both giggled as they made their way to the park. They parked, paid for their admission, then proceeded through a long tunnel. When they came out of the tunnel, Lizzy thought it reminded her of Dorothy's house that had just landed in Oz and everything suddenly turned to color when she opened the door. The sights and smells put their senses into overdrive.

"Brad, can we get something to eat first? I'm starving."

"Sure, what did you have in mind?"

"I saw on the map, right by the Garden Stage, there is a restaurant called Pagoda, which serves lunch or dinner on one side and delectable desserts on the other side. Then we can have our cake and lunch too." Lizzy grinned.

"Lizzy, you are so funny. I can see the little girl coming out of you as we speak."

Brad and Lizzy both reverted to their youth and were having so much fun they barely noticed when the day had passed. It was nine forty-five, and the fireworks were scheduled to go off in fifteen minutes. The temperature had dropped, and the air had become cool, so they put on the hoodies they'd brought and found a spot to sit by the river.

Brad wrapped his arms around Lizzy as the fireworks lit up the sky and reflected off of the river. They both were elated and couldn't have imagined a better day.

Later, they made their way to Brad's car and waited for the traffic jam to subside. They recapped the day's events.

"What was your favorite of the day, Brad?"

"It was the fireworks. It reminded me of how I feel every time I see you."

"Oh, Brad." They shared a passionate kiss before they headed back to Verona.

CHAPTER 24

The trees had budded, the mountains had pockets of green, and spring was in the air, the day the church reopened. The pews had returned home, as though they knew they had accomplished their goal. Even though the pews hadn't really orchestrated anything, God did—their mere existence had brought Brad and Lizzy together. Brad and Lizzy had been inseparable for the last two months. They had seen new things and explored new places. Their relationship had graduated into a deep love, and there was even talk of marriage. They were convinced they were made for each other, and that their meeting had been a divine intervention.

It seemed like many things had changed course after the pub had gotten those pews. Bonnie's son Ian, whose bone had healed without any complication. Ian's brother, Tony, and his friends did a total turnaround and were coming to the church at the pub regularly. Bonnie and David had started to date and were building a strong relationship. Teddy Summer, Suzie Q and

her family, the Daily juice guys, Bill Wells, Bob Gooding, and Brian Smart—all had started attending church
also. The church numbers had grown. None of this
would have happened without those pews being moved
to the pub.

The church looked brand new. Except for the different color walls and carpet, the congregation probably wouldn't have noticed any differences. There were
more than one hundred and fifty in attendance today.
There was a portable spa pool set up front for the bap-
tisms that were going to take place before the service.
Today, Lizzy, Bonnie, David, and Tony all were going to
make their public professions of faith and be baptized.

David, with a long white robe, was the first one to
enter the water to join Brad, who wore waist waders
underneath his robe. Brad looked at David. "Do you,
David, take Jesus as your personal Savior, and will you
follow Him for the rest of your days?"

David answered with choked-back tears, "Yes, I do,
and I will."

Brad placed a towel over David's face while he held
his nose. Brad supported his back and said, "I baptize
you in the name of the Father, the Son, and the Holy
Spirit," as he submerged David backward, covering him
with the water. As David ascended, the whole congregation clapped. David gave Brad a hug before exiting
the pool.

After David came Bonnie. After Bonnie was her son Tony. Lizzy was last.

Lizzy thought her heart was beating like a rabbit's. She was so excited, but she wanted to save every moment of the baptism in her memory. She, too, received applause from the congregation when she came out of the water. Brad said, "Before you leave, as you place your trust in the Lord, will you put your trust in me as well? Together we will collectively trust the Lord." Brad looked deep into Lizzy's brown eyes. "Will you, Lizzy Murphy, make me the happiest man on earth and be my wife?" He took out a small box, opened it, and pulled out a ring.

Lizzy looked at Brad, then at the ring, then back to Brad. "Yes!" she exclaimed.

The congregation erupted into bigger applause than before. They kissed as a young couple, Rick and Donna, started to play the piano and sing "When God Made You." Lizzy and Brad were excited, and there wasn't one dry eye under the steeple.

While they were singing, Brad quickly took off his wet robe and rubber waders, straightened out his clothes, and combed his hair. Lizzy went into a small room where there were changing stalls. Apparently, Bonnie was already done because the room was empty. Little did Lizzy know that Bonnie had known about the proposal. So, Bonnie had quickly gone back to the sanctuary to join David and Tony to watch it take place. Lizzy took off her wet robe and clothes and changed into the dry clothes that she had brought. She did a quick blow-dry of her hair with the hairdryer, then pulled it up into a ponytail. She euphorically made her way back to a pew in the last row while the couple was finishing their song.

Brad made his way to the altar and thanked the couple for the most perfect song for this day. He then, customarily, started his prayer, preceded by asking the congregation to turn to Genesis 2:20–24. Then he said, "Today's sermon is entitled, 'Loneliness versus Being Alone.' And why God never intended for us to be alone."

Brad then read from the Bible, starting at Genesis 2:20: "'So the man gave names to all the livestock, the birds in the sky and all the wild animals. But for Adam no suitable helper was found. So the LORD God caused the man to fall into a deep sleep; and while he was sleeping, he took one of the man's ribs and then closed up the place with flesh. Then the LORD God made a woman from the rib he had taken out of the man, and he brought her to the man. The man said, This is now bone of my bone and flesh of my flesh; she shall be called woman, for she was taken out of man. That is why a man leaves his father and mother and is united to his wife, and they become one flesh.'"

Brad continued by saying, "Now, you who are singles who are currently alone and like it that way, what does this have to with loneliness versus being alone? Loneliness is when you feel that there is no one in the world who wants to understand you, but when you feel alone, you're really never alone.

"In Joshua 1:51, God promises that He will never leave you or forsake you. Then He sent proof by sending His Son, who promised that not only are He and our Father going to be with us now, but forevermore.

"So, when you feel that overwhelming sense loneliness, take the solitude and take the time to be alone with the Lord through prayer and reading the scriptures. I guarantee you won't feel that loneliness anymore."

Brad continued his sermon and then ended with an invitation to the altar and prayer. Before dismissing everyone, he reminded them that there was a welcome-back buffet in the kitchen and invited them to please stay.

Lizzy had prepared a reception meal after the service to welcome people back. It was a light-fare lunch with three tables set up, each with finger sandwiches, potato salad, macaroni salad, and fruit. Lizzy had also made three hand-crafted sheet cakes. She had piped yellow roses on them and letters that said, "Welcome Back." She had practiced for years to refine her cake tastes, frostings, and piping skills. She would come full circle imagining the beautifully designed wedding cakes she wanted to make. While most women dreamed of their wedding dresses, Lizzy Googled cakes. At the reception, everyone came up to Brad and Lizzy, congratulating them for their engagement, and not one person failed to mention how delicious the cakes were.

The Landrys mentioned that they felt they had been a real part of their engagement because they had been there at the inception. They, too, complimented the cakes. They suggested to Lizzy that she should put a price on her special cakes and sell them.

Lizzy asked Cindy, "Did you know about the proposal today?"

Cindy giggled. "Um... Maybe... Yes."

"You are going to get it tomorrow!" Lizzy laughed. "You are a great secret keeper, which is a good thing."

Lizzy said the same thing to Bonnie, with the same response. Bonnie, David, and Tony helped clean up the church before they departed. When Lizzy and Brad finally found themselves alone, Lizzy took a real look at her ring. It was a one-carat solitaire diamond surrounded by rubies. "Where did you get this beautiful ring? I love it—and I love you."

"It was my mom's ring. Since I was an only child, she left it to me before she died. And I am sure that if she were alive, she definitely would want you to have it. She would have loved you like I do. I feel sad that she's not here to see it all."

"Maybe she is watching from heaven." Lizzy felt sad about her parents not being there as well.

"I am so happy that you said yes to my proposal today. It would have been really embarrassing if you'd said no." His laughing now turned serious. "Now I have another proposal that I want you to consider. I know how much you have felt trapped at the pub, and that you have wanted to have a wedding reception venue. I have been talking to the Landrys, and we are in agreement that this area has a need for a youth center. There are many kids in Verona and Oakmont who, quite frankly, don't have anything to do after school, especially if they are not involved in extracurricular activities. With this idle time, as you know, they end up making wrong choices and go down the wrong path.

"So, the first part of the proposal is that the Landrys have agreed to contribute fifty thousand dollars as seed money to convert the pub into a youth center. The center would be open after school until a bus took the kids home at seven, Monday through Friday. How this would work is that the church would take their donation, make the necessary improvements to the pub to meet State regulations, and then the church would pay you to rent the space and sponsor it. We agreed that would be enough to offset the loss in the revenue that the pub generated. We would have different professionals come in for career counseling for the kids. We would hire you to oversee the place and furnish nutritional snacks for the kids after school. Perhaps you could even give some cooking and baking classes since you are certified throughout the county. You would need a background check and CPR and first aid certification. Of course, I will be there for mentoring and to expose the kids to the Bible. We already have two volunteers, David and Bonnie. Tony wants to help too. Cindy used to be an art teacher before she married Michael, and she wants to volunteer to teach art classes. She also thinks that some of her friends could teach creative writing, acting, and crafts."

Brad took a deep breath while Lizzy listened intently. "The second part of the proposal is my idea alone. I have an inheritance from my grandfather. I want to use it to convert the garage into a wedding reception hall. The youth program will leave the whole place open on the weekends so that you could utilize the pub to handle the receptions. I think you would be great and so successful. I believe in you, Lizzy Murphy, and I want you to be the happiest woman alive. We could do all this work over the summer months for the youth center. The wedding hall would then take six months, with the first wedding reception taking place being our own, at Christmastime."

Lizzy smiled through her tears. "Yes, I love the idea, and I love you. I am the happiest woman in the world."

CHAPTER 25

B rad and Lizzy went on the attack to convert the pub into a youth center/wedding reception hall. They knew they were racing against the clock, because they wanted to allow enough wiggle room, in case they experienced unexpected obstacles. They strategically put a list together of their own priorities, then melded them together in one list. They knew it would be a team effort and they joked by calling it "a true test of their compatibility." If they survived, it would be a true indication of their blissful future together.

Michael Landry said he had a good architect friend on Hulton Road. His name was Jerry Jenkins. His firm was the one that had designed the high-end condos located in Oakmont, where the old Edgewater Steel Company had stood. Jerry owned a contracting company as well, so he should be able to do it all of the necessary work. Michael made an appointment for Friday morning to meet with him.

Michael said, "I think for the most part, there won't be any major structural issues, even with changing some of the entrances. Most of the job would be cosmetic remodeling for the youth center. Jerry will be able to give you a projected cost of the project, and his estimates supposedly are right on the money. We go way back, and he agrees about the need for the youth center and a place to host wedding receptions. He said he would be willing to do it for close to his cost."

Brad went to the State to obtain the appropriate licenses. The State wanted to make an initial inspection for safety before issuing a license. They also recommended a program from Governor Wolf, which was an initiative to educate the staff of after-school programs. Brad signed up Lizzy, David, Bonnie, and himself for the next class taking place the next month at the convention center downtown.

Lizzy, likewise, did research on catering and liquor licenses. She found out that her food license through Allegheny County was sufficient. If the wedding party wanted alcohol, they could supply their own, as long as they obtained it from a state liquor store, although she wasn't going to encourage that. Lizzy was surprised when she found out that because there were a limited number of liquor licenses issued by the State, a liquor license in Pittsburgh was selling for seventy-five thousand dollars. She thought she would use that money instead to pay down the pub's loan and refinance it. That would save her over a thousand dollars a month.

In their discussions about the center, Brad and Lizzy felt that keeping the kids safe was paramount. Locked doors were essential, not only to keep the kids in, but to keep unwanted guests out. So, they decided to add another alarmed emergency exit by the bathrooms and add a buzzer to the entrance door. They decided to make it a non-electronic zone, so sadly they thought David would need to wand the kids with a metal detector as they came in; he could say it was to detect any electronic devices, but it would also be a backup for all metal objects. The kids would have to place their phones in a lockbox, so they made sure there was access to a landline, in case it was needed.

They decided to place an accordion wall to partition the bar area off, with a door to the kitchen, and also an accordion wall between the garage and bar so that the flow would be from the front to the back of the building. These would be locked for the center hours, but they could be opened when used for wedding receptions. They also decided to remove the pool table and replace it with a collapsible Ping-Pong table so it could be moved during a wedding reception. They were going to keep the big screen TV and add a Blu-Ray for Christian movies. They removed the electronic dartboards and replaced them with cabinets for supplies. They decided to keep the jukebox but only have it play contemporary Christian music, like LeCrae, Casting Crowns, Mercy Me, Newsboys, and other similar artists.

Brad, Lizzy, and Michael Landry met with the architect, Jerry Jenkins, on Friday as scheduled. Jerry brought his laptop and showed them a virtual schematic of his proposed plans. He felt that most of the center would need whitewash paint, contemporary floor coverings, and necessary safety features. He wanted to add a split entry with two distinct doors, one going into the reception area and one door for the center. He thought a royal-blue awning over both would be a nice added touch. That should leave enough money for bigger round tables, built-in cabinets, and supplies that the center would need.

The reception area would include an expanded kitchen area, more bathrooms, drywall, and recessed lighting, with a crystal chandelier over the wedding party's table. He felt that waterproof flooring would be the best bet, because it also would be good material for dancing and would hold up to the traffic. He showed the area with twenty ten-seat tables, the wedding party table, a dance floor. and an elevated bandstand.

The price seemed reasonable to Brad and Lizzy, and they gave him the go-ahead.

Lizzy would then go on the hunt for tables, chairs, dishes, stemware, and silverware. She needed more prep stands for the expanded kitchen, along with more refrigeration and convection ovens and an industrial dishwasher. Lizzy thought to herself she had already done enough dishes by hand to last a lifetime, so the dishwasher was mandatory. She didn't have to worry about money at this point, and it wasn't an issue because of Brad's inheritance.

Brad and Lizzy decided that they would reside in the apartment over the pub, but they hoped someday to have a home with some land and horses. Lizzy reached out to Vickie, who was so excited for her. She said she wanted to come visit and help pick out her wedding dress, and she would be more than happy to perform her matron-of-honor responsibilities. She volunteered her kids to be the ring bearer and flower girl. Vickie and her husband, Don, made plans to come over in August, before the kids had to go back to school. Vickie insisted on paying for all the flowers, the band, and a horse and carriage to take them from the church to the pub, and she arranged shuttles for the rest of the people from the church. They were very excited for Lizzy, and they were looking forward to meeting Brad. Of course, they thought the youth center and wedding reception hall were wonderful ideas. They couldn't wait to see everything.

Progress on both projects were on schedule. Tony and his friends whitewashed the barnwood, which immediately brightened the room. They found some contemporary artwork and bright-colored rugs to place under the tables. It started to look like a cool place for teens to hang out. Tony started to take on some leadership responsibilities. He and David started to really bond as they took on the work together.

Lizzy was able to keep the pub open during the summer, which gave her the opportunity to say good-bye to all of her "summer people." Everyone thought the youth center and reception hall were much needed, and they were happy for her, although they were going to miss the view. They all wished her much luck in her new venture and happiness with her future husband.

The grand opening for the youth center was scheduled for August twenty-ninth. Lizzy's sister, Vickie, thought it best to come the week before to visit with her family. They arrived early Saturday, August twenty-second, and got a room at a local hotel. Lizzy had arranged the night before, Friday, August twenty-first, to be a free customer appreciation and farewell buffet for the patrons of the pub. It was bittersweet. The pub had been around for almost fifty-nine years. There had been some great memories forged there, but the idea to give back to the community and form new memories was equally exciting. There was an abundance of hugs and tears as people left that evening.

Lizzy, although exhausted from the night before, couldn't wait to see Vickie, Don, Colin, and Katherine.

They were going to meet at Casey's for breakfast. Then the guys were going to take the kids to the Pittsburgh Zoo, and the girls were going shopping for a bridal gown and bridesmaid dresses at the Magic Moment Bridal Studio.

Lizzy and Vickie hugged for a long time and spent most of the breakfast going down memory lane. They had forgotten how much they loved each other, and it was apparent that they were tearing down walls that they hadn't realized had grown so tall. Brad and Don were getting along great, too, and they both seemed to be well-versed in an array of subjects. Cindy stopped by to meet Vickie and told her what a special sister she had in Lizzy. Vickie agreed and said, "Thanks."

Don and Brad left the restaurant in Don's rental car with the kids, while Lizzy and Vickie headed to the bridal shop.

"I really like Brad. You can tell by the way he looks at you that he's madly in love with you. I am so happy for you, baby sister. I am sorry I haven't been as close as I should have. I suppose I felt like Dad liked you better, but in reality, I was just so sad I didn't get to spend more time with them while they were alive. I just thought they were going to be here longer."

"We both felt things about each other that probably had no merit, but that was then and this is now. I love you, big sissy, and I always will. I think we don't know when the good Lord is going to take us home, and we should never forget what is precious and true and never stop saying we love each other while we can."

Lizzy and Vickie fell in love with the first wedding dress Lizzy tried on. Lizzy hadn't noticed with all that was going on that she had lost a lot of weight. The dress was form-fitted with the right amount of satin and lace. Lizzy truly looked like a princess. They both agreed on a veil that would fit around an updo. They collectively decided on ruby-red velvet bridesmaids dresses. The kids would have matching outfits. The men would wear black with red cummerbunds and bowties. They picked out red rose invitations, napkins, and accessories.

Brad and Don hit it off famously. Brad tried the intellectual route to explain to Don about Jesus. Don was raised Catholic and he knew of Jesus, but he didn't personally know Him. He told Brad that he would take a second look and seriously wanted to learn more. He told Brad that a lot of the doctors had been praying with patients and had found that patients with faith healed quicker and had fewer complications.

The weekend went by all too fast, but Lizzy and Vickie promised to be in constant communication to make sure the wedding—and their sisterly love—were perfect.

CHAPTER 26

The grand opening of Verona's Youth Center finally arrived. It was a sunny seventy-five-degree day, with a nice breeze. Brad and Lizzy were growing closer to each other by working through the problems that arose. Brad bought a used van to pick up kids from Riverview Middle and High Schools. If the numbers grew, the schools would then furnish school buses. Brad dealt with the state, county, and municipalities as far as permits and zoning went. He got some state grants, which enabled them not only to enhance the programs but also to pay for field trips to the zoo and the Carnegie Museum of Art. Michael Landry had been a pivotal part of the process due to his connections, so now the center was being dedicated in Landry's name.

Lizzy handled the remodeling process, working closely with Jerry Jenkins on both projects. He told her not to worry about her wedding reception and promised that the facility would definitely be done by Christmas. Lizzy dealt with the schools where Cindy had connections, because she was involved with the PTA. She had secured the school board and principal's trust by showing them a PowerPoint presentation to demonstrate how the program statistically would improve the area and attitudes of the schoolkids themselves.

David and Tony became inseparable and developed a sort of father/son relationship. David's PTSD evaporated, and he would say, "God brought me back from the dead. He brushed me off, and now I am better than before." He and Bonnie were now engaged, and they wanted to be the second wedding party to use Lizzy's new facility.

Lizzy and Brad met at the center to go over the last-minute details, because the ribbon-cutting and ceremony was to take place at noon.

"Good morning, sunshine," Brad said before he gave Lizzy a passionate kiss.

Lizzy replied with a bright smile, "Good morning. I have to admit, I am very nervous about this whole event. Who did you say was coming again?"

"You don't need to be nervous. You have done a fabulous job, but most important, God is with us, as you know when we have felt Him during our prayers." Lizzy nodded but still couldn't shake off the butterflies.

"We have confirmation that the mayors of Oakmont and Verona are coming. Most of the Riverview school board members are coming, and the principals and assistant principals of both the middle and high school are attending. A majority of teachers and a boatload of parents are also coming to check us out." He added, "Oh yeah, KDKA is sending the reporter who did our original story to cover the event."

Now Lizzy wished she hadn't asked, because knowing the higher-ups in the community and the news stations were coming only made her more nervous. She tried to blow it off by talking about the weather. "We are so lucky that the weather is going to cooperate and it's going to be a beautiful day." How many golf carts and people do we have to shuttle from the church?"

"We rented four carts, and David and some of his buddies from the VA are going to help drive people back and forth from the church. But I imagine some people will be walking."

"Do you think we will have enough room?" Lizzy asked in a concerned voice.

"Don't forget we are going to open the slider to the deck just for today, and since we are only serving cookies and punch, there won't be a need for additional chairs." He looked at her with endearing eyes. "I love you so much, Lizzy. You are everything I was looking for and more. You haven't made one complaint through this process, which would have brought most people to their knees. I feel like I hit the jackpot with you. I am the happiest man in the world." This was followed by another longer, passionate kiss. Lizzy knew that she hadn't crumbled because she had spent many years at the pub learning problem-solving. Complaining never accomplished a thing. She had a whole new direction through the love of God and Brad, which gave her not only purposeful confidence, but most of their problems disappeared and they trusted God for the rest.

The ribbon had been placed under the blue awning. It was secure, and there were three large scissors, one for the Landrys, one for the mayors, and one for Brad and Lizzy to use to cut the ribbon. There was a twenty-foot banner that read, "WELCOME TO VERONA'S YOUTH CENTER," and underneath that, "SPONSORED BY THE LANDRYS AND THE FIRST BAPTIST CHURCH OF VERONA." Lizzy had used a helium canister to inflate fifty black and gold balloons in the school colors and had them located inside. Outside, on the ribbon, were tied eighteen black and gold, and eighteen red, white, and blue, balloons, so when the ribbon was cut they would float upward while the Riverview Band played "God Bless America."

People started to show up early. Officer Lange had volunteered to direct traffic toward the church even though there were directional signs. Arch Road could be complicated. Brad got permission from the owners of the empty lot across the street to park the band bus and allow for official parking for those who had special passes, such as the mayors, school officials, and the KDKA news station, which Officer Lange coordinated. Michael and Cindy Landry showed up, and as always, pitched in as needed.

Lizzy gave Cindy a big hug. "There are ten extra-large trays of cookies left in the kitchen. I left a display there to give the people a look at the cooking program we are going to teach to the youth, and there's extra punch in the fridge. I thought between the two of us, we should be able to keep the tables full." Cindy nodded her head.

Cindy had written a whole curriculum and had put into motion many programs that filled the calendar, including cooking and baking lessons. She had made up a trifold brochure handout to showcase them, and she had put in their mission statement, from Proverbs 22:6: "Train a child in the way he should go, and when he is old he will not turn away from it." The four of them had started a foundation, vowing it to be privately funded, and a call to "invest in our future by investing in our future generations." Each table had been staged to show the different activities for art, writing tablets, fun mind games, theater props, and playwrights. The jukebox was on a low volume playing contemporary Christian music, and the Ping-Pong table was removed easily for the Friday socials and dancing.

Bonnie and the girls from the shop, Crystal and Maggie, volunteered as welcome hostesses, encouraging people to pick up a pamphlet, cookies, and drinks. Lizzy came over to them. "First of all, I want to say that you all look beautiful." They had all put on pretty dresses and were all made up, including their hair. "And thank you so much for your help today, and for your help in making this day happen. I love you all like sisters." With that, they all did a group hug.

Lizzy couldn't believe how many people showed up. She wondered where all the people had come from. The parking lot was full, and the band was playing patriotic music. She also thought, "Thank goodness it wasn't the full band, or there wouldn't have been enough room." The wheels in Lizzy's head were spinning so fast she thought her head might just fly off.

Finally, the mayors, the Landrys, Brad, and Lizzy stood behind the ribbon facing the crowd and the news cameras. The mayor gave thanks to them, and in gratitude handed them the keys to the cities. There was no shortage of applause.

Brad stepped up to the microphone and first thanked the Landrys for their contributions that had made this dream come true. Then he said, "I want everyone to know that my fiancée, Lizzy, and I felt a calling to do this for God and the community. We aren't replacing you parents. We are an additional positive reinforcement. We are the extra encouragement these kids need. We believe every kid has their own unique gifts from God that, when tapped, will build their self-esteem. That can lead to confidence, not only in school, but confidence that will follow them for the rest of their lives."

He paused. "We are not replacing you teachers, either. We are only trying to supplement the great work you do. We know you work extremely hard. Our goals are to enhance that and add another dimension to what the kids have already gotten from you.

"Lastly, since we are Christian-based, the kids will have the option to study the Bible. We want them to have a choice to look at creation versus evolution and let them discern their own opinions. When the kids learn to think independently, they become leaders, not followers. When they learn to believe with their own minds, this creates a passion that no one can take away."

There was a big applause, and Brad said, "Thank you. After the ribbon cutting, there are refreshments inside. After looking at the facility, you can go out to the deck and circle around. Please take a pamphlet that will explain our mission and show some of the programs we plan on conducting at the center. Again, thank you for your support, and God bless you."

The Landrys, Brad, Lizzy, and the mayors all stood behind the ribbon, grabbed one of the three keys, and in unison cut the ribbon. After that, the balloons took to flight, the band played "God Bless America," and the people formed a line to enter the building. Brad, Lizzy, the Landrys, and the mayors shook people's hands as they entered. There wasn't one negative remark, but gratuitous thanks from all.

The day couldn't have gone any better. It was a total success. All the people who were left after the cleanup got a surprise invitation from the Landrys to come to Casey's, where they had reserved the back room for a free dinner and drinks. Some people hopped into the van that read "Verona's Youth Center," some got into their cars, and they all went to the restaurant with a great sense of accomplishment and hope for the future of the local youth.

CHAPTER 27

The youth center grew in popularity, with about the same amount of kids coming from Oakmont and Verona. There were twelve regular after-school students and four who would pop in now and then. The kids were an eclectic group from the ages of thirteen to sixteen, and there were a few more boys than girls. The feedback from the parents was favorable. The parents who could afford to were making unsolicited donations, feeling that their kids were benefiting tremendously from the program and they wanted to keep it going. Most of the kids opted into the Bible study that Brad conducted every day. Only a few had ever heard the story of Jesus. One day they watched a movie called *Is Genesis History?* It was a 2017 documentary that used scientific facts to prove the origins of earth that produced truths found in the book of Genesis in the Bible. After the Bible study, most of the kids gravitated toward the arts, although the kids loved it when Lizzy taught cooking, where they learned about food safety first followed by baking and learning to make pizza from scratch. There were a couple of kids who were more active and enjoyed Ping-Pong and other games.

Lizzy grew particularly close to one of the girls named Maria. She reminded her of herself at that pre-pubescent age. Maria was a Hispanic twelve-year-old, in seventh grade at Riverview Middle School, and she was struggling with her weight. Lizzy remembered how unkind some of the kids had been to her because of her own weight. But she thought the kids were much more brutal these days, using another tier of bullying through social media.

She felt empathy toward Maria and felt the need to give her some extra armor to help her combat the insecurity she was experiencing. Lizzy knew her parents were hardworking and loving, but she knew that couldn't always overcome the weight of peer pressure that took over at that age. She was bound and determined not to let Maria cave in because of that pressure. She wanted to instill in her the fact that she was special, and that God loved her just the way she was. They soon developed a special relationship.

Maria would always come into the center and go straight to Lizzy, who would take her and whoever else wanted to go to the kitchen to prepare the snacks. However, it soon boiled down to it being just Maria preparing snacks every day. Lizzy would start by handing

Maria the clipboard and have her go out and do a head-count by placing a checkmark by each name. Lizzy explained that some of the kids had food allergies, so she taught Maria to read labels, which also covertly taught her about calorie counting.

Lizzy taught Maria about staying away from refined sugars, carbohydrates, and GMOs, and she tried to use only fresh ingredients when available. Some of the kids' favorites were ants on a log, pigs in a blanket, banana bread muffins, sliced avocados with a sweet casicum dip, and edamame in a soy curry sauce. They would Google "nutritional snacks for teens" and make a sort of game out of it. They also were honing their own recipes for smoothies to offer instead of plain juice.

Today, Lizzy already had plates ready for the kids with ants on a log. They were celery sticks with peanut butter, except two had cream cheese, with a row of raisins on top. She had made and poured the pineapple banana smoothies into cups.

"Buenos tardes, Maria." Lizzy gave her a big hug and a kiss on her soft cheek.

Maria looked puzzled. "Aren't we going to make something together?"

"Yes, we are. I decided since we are going to go to the Carnegie Museum of Art tomorrow for a field trip, we are going to bake gluten-free brownies and wrap them up to take with us." Lizzy was excited to take Maria to the museum because she really gravitated toward Cindy's teaching of art. Cindy had up to this point just taught chalk, oil pastels, and markers, but after the trip she was planning on bringing out the paints and brushes. Cindy had made mention to Lizzy that she saw remarkable talent in Maria.

"Go take the snacks out while I get the ingredients ready for the gluten-free brownies, then come back to the kitchen and let's have ourselves some fun!" Lizzy had gotten the recipe online, downloaded it, and printed it out for them to follow:

INGREDIENTS
- 1½ cups superfine sugar
- ½ cup unsalted butter
- ½ teaspoon salt
- 1 teaspoon gluten-free vanilla extract
- ¾ cup Dutch-process cocoa powder
- 3 large eggs
- ¾ cup gluten-free all-purpose flour
- 1 teaspoon baking powder
- 1 cup chocolate chips

INSTRUCTIONS

1. Preheat the oven to 350 degrees. Grease an 8-inch square pan.

2. Place the sugar, butter, and salt in a saucepan. Heat over medium heat, stirring until the butter melts and the mixture lightens in color. This step helps melt the sugar, which will give the brownies a shiny crust.
3. Transfer the mixture to a bowl. Blend in the vanilla and cocoa, then add the eggs and mix until shiny.
4. Blend in the flour and baking powder, then stir in the chocolate chips.
5. Pour batter into a greased pan, spreading it to the edges.
6. Bake the brownies for 33 to 38 minutes, insert a toothpick in the center and when it comes out clean, remove from the oven.
7. Let the brownies cool for at least 15 minutes before cutting.

Maria came back after delivering the afternoon snacks to the other kids. Lizzy reminded her to wash her hands while singing the song "Happy Birthday," long enough to kill the germs. Lizzy taught her to double the recipe, and after they baked them, Lizzy and Maria proceeded to put the cooled cut brownies into plastic baggies. The brownies looked perfect. They placed the wrapped brownies in the basket for the next day's trip to the Carnegie Museum of Art.

"You did a great job, Maria. Why don't you go and do a little artwork before the bus comes to take you home?"

Maria gave Lizzy a hug and kiss. She felt happy and had a sense of accomplishment. She left the kitchen and joined some of the others at Cindy's art table, where they were collectively working on a mandala, so she joined in and started to happily color.

The van was buzzing as it headed downtown to the museum. Lizzy thought the kids were excited to see the great displays of art, but she had a notion that their excitement could have been a result of the brownies and juice they had consumed on the way there.

The museum had provided the group with a guide to explain the different eras of painting styles. Each era was separated by rooms. They walked through Ancient Classical Art, Medieval Art, Renaissance, Renaissance to Neoclassicism, Romanticism, Romanticism to Modern Art, Modern Art, and Contemporary. Lizzy and Brad both agreed they like the Impressionist art the best, including Monet. The Carnegie brought a lot of culture to Pittsburgh, as did the Heinz family, making Pittsburgh ranked as one of the top cultural destinations in the world thanks to their contributions. Lizzy and Brad were so proud of the kids as they listened intently and their behavior was stellar. The kids' conversations on the way back were a lively commentary of what they had seen and liked best. The day went perfect, and when the last of the kids were dropped off, Lizzy and Brad went to grab a bite at Panera.

The main topics while they were eating were about their wedding plans. But they also discussed the church's annual Christmas story that the kids performed. Much to Brad's surprise, most of the youth center kids wanted to participate too. If not with the acting, they wanted to help make the scenery. It did Brad's heart good to see all the kids working together to make the stable. The mother who had previously made the costumes agreed to make more and add a few more animals as well.

Then there was an even bigger surprise when four of the older kids, two boys and two girls, had been practicing an a capella rendition that the group the Pentatonix had made popular, "Mary, Did You Know?" They performed for the other kids, and everyone agreed it was fabulous. Brad asked them if they would sing it at church on Christmas Eve. They said they would like that. They had to check with their parents first, but they felt it would be fine.

The next day at the center was the day Cindy was giving the first lesson on acrylic painting. She thought it was perfect timing, while the art museum was still fresh in the kids' minds. She made a display of a bowl with fruit in it, set it on a lace tablecloth, and added two pewter candlesticks. She showed them how to mix colors on a palette and make shades by mixing black and white into the colors. She taught them the correct way to hold the brushes and how to make different strokes. She handed the kids some paint paper, paper towels, and a cup of water to rinse their brushes in between different colors.

She decided to give them free range and see what they would come up with and who she thought might have talent. Cindy always liked this part the best, watching the kids begin with some intimidation and then, like a flower, open up and bloom. She would hang around if any of the kids had any questions, but like a good book, she didn't want to spoil the ending and peek at their work before they were finished.

Cindy went into the kitchen. "Lizzy, you have to come out here. There is something I want to show you." She took Lizzy over to the table where all the kids were standing behind Maria, watching her put the final touches on her painting. Lizzy made her way closer, so that she could see her painting.

"Oh my God, Maria, that is beautiful!" Lizzy exclaimed. "It looks like you could take that apple right off the picture and eat it." The painting indeed looked like a master had painted it. It had dimension, shadowing, perfect colors, and looked more like a photo than a painting.

All the kids were amazed. They told her how awesome Maria was, and the compliments just keep pouring onto her.

Cindy said to Lizzy, "Just look at Maria's pride, to have all that affirmation from others."

"I do believe that we have found Maria's gift. Thank You, God."

CHAPTER 28

Things were going along famously well at the center, and Brad and Lizzy remained inseparable. They booked their honeymoon to LaCabana in Aruba, leaving the day after Christmas. Lizzy was so excited. Except for going to WVU, she had never been out of the state and she had never flown before. They made the decision to abstain and not consummate their marriage until the honeymoon. They both definitely wanted to have two kids, starting right away, and they would laugh, saying that they didn't want to show up at the kids' schools with "white hair."

Vickie flew over by herself in October. Brad, Lizzy, and Vickie went over the guest list and whittled it down to one hundred and fifty guests. They discovered all the people were local except for Brad's dad and Vickie and her family, so they collectively decided that a Christmas Day wedding was possible, if it took place in the evening. So, the final decision was made that the wedding would be on December 25th at 6:30 p.m. They immediately bought some Christmas-themed paper and sent a "hold this date" mailer to everyone on the list.

Brad and Lizzy began a bridal registry at a website called The Knot, as well as Macy's and Bed, Bath, and Beyond. Vickie couldn't believe how well Brad and Lizzy got along, with total agreement across the board on what they wanted and what patterns they liked. She would affectionately call them "peas in a pod," and while laughing, even say that they must "share a brain."

Vickie took charge, with Brad and Lizzy's approval, and ordered the rest of the things needed for the wedding. She insisted on paying for everything, not because she had to but because she wanted to. She arranged for an upscale caterer to come. They would provide the food, dishes, silverware, tablecloths, and napkins, the ruby-red satin chair covers, and a waitstaff. Vickie decided to have etched stemware with their names and date engraved, so that everyone could take them home as a remembrance of the occasion.

She ordered all the flowers, which were red roses with baby's breath. That would be for all the bridesmaids, groomsmen, the lantern candles for the church, the table centerpieces, the wedding party table, her daughter's flower girl rose petals, and a birdcage for the wedding cards. Then she ordered red and white poinsettias to be placed throughout the pub and the church.

She arranged a horse and buggy to take the couple from the church to the reception, and she lined up a well-known photographer as well. Then the three of them decided on a DJ, and Brad and Lizzy selected the music. They decided they were only to serve soft drinks and Korbel champagne for the toast. The invitations were embossed with delicate raised roses, and they ordered a matching guestbook and cocktail napkins.

Vickie left after a weeklong visit, but not before she made sure that Brad and Lizzy would come and spend Thanksgiving with them in Bucks County, which arrived before they knew it. Brad and Lizzy were taken in by the beauty of Don and Vickie's place. Their house had actually been featured in an article in Better Homes and Gardens. Brad and Lizzy could see why. Lizzy found herself no longer feeling jealous or envious, but truly happy for her sister. She felt only love now, and she was kicking herself for being so petty in the past.

The invitations were mailed, the dresses fitted, and the poinsettias brought in early to decorate the church. Lizzy said, "They have a short life anyway, so they might as well get Vickie's money's worth."

The kids were doing a great job on the scenery for the play. Cindy had brought in a stained glass to make ornaments, so that the kids could give them to their parents for Christmas. Lizzy thought Christmas cookies would be an appropriate cooking lesson to teach the kids. She furnished cookie tins as an additional gift. They had so much fun decorating them.

Lizzy made list upon list as Christmas approached. She ordered and received ruby-red Swarovski earrings and necklace sets to give to the bridesmaids. She had bought embroidered dopp kits for Brad's groomsmen. She couldn't think of anything she had forgotten. In fact, she was having difficulty thinking at all. Thank God that Vickie was there to keep her focused. Brad's dad, Vickie, Don, and the kids arrived on December twenty-second. They coordinated their flights and stayed at the same hotel so that they only needed to rent one car.

Vickie made sure Lizzy understood that they were going to celebrate Christmas when they got home. Colin, ten years old, knew there was no Santa, but Katherine, at eight years old, thought Santa's gifts would be waiting for her when she got home. Don and Vickie had bought the kids iPads for Christmas to entertain them while they were being shuffled around and somewhat ignored during the wedding protocol. Vickie said that there shouldn't be any gift exchanges, as the wedding was the ultimate gift anyway.

School ended on Tuesday, December twenty-second, so the caterers were coming on the twenty-third to set up the tables and chairs. They would be back at four o'clock on Christmas day to prepare the food. The etched stemware sat in big boxes. Lizzy had already run them through the dishwasher.

The gang from the pub went together and bought a thirty-foot tree and decorated it for the deck. All the tables and chairs were sold and off the deck by then, so the tree looked pristine standing alone. It looked so lovely through the glass, lit up at night, with the river and mountains in the backdrop. Lizzy truly appreciated it, and she thought it was the perfect gift and wedding photo opportunity.

Lizzy made three layers of different-sized cakes and froze them. One was marbled, one was chocolate, and the bottom was vanilla-flavored. She would assemble and decorate them early on the twenty-fourth. She purchased a fountain with stairs going to the second layer and four plastic bridesmaids dressed in ruby-red dresses and four groomsmen in black with red cummerbunds and bowties. On top were the bride and groom standing in front of a cross. She decided to put red roses between the layers, on top of white buttercream frosting.

All the flowers arrived on the twenty-fourth, which was perfect because the Christmas service was that evening. They had candle lanterns with roses and bows attached to the pews, a beautiful centerpiece they could use for the altar, and all those poinsettias looked so beautiful for the Christmas service and then the wedding. There was the manger for the kids' performance. As the people left, they said the service was "absolutely and completely perfect."

The rehearsal dinner was at seven o'clock at Casey's. The restaurant was closed, so they had the place to themselves. Cindy brought in caterers, as well. She thought since she and her husband, the best man, were in the wedding, that was the best option. The whole wedding party and their families were there, including the Landrys; the matron of honor, Vickie; and the bridesmaids, Bonnie, Cindy, and Suzie Q and her family. The groomsmen—David, Don, and Carlos—and Carlos's family were there as well. The ushers were Tony and Teddy. With Vickie's kids as the ring bearer and flower girl, and Brad's dad, there were twenty-five people total at the dinner.

After the dinner, there were many toasts, like "match made in heaven" and "perfect couple," and then they went over to the church for a final walk-through.

CHAPTER 29

The wedding evening finally arrived. The air was brisk with expected snow, but luckily no significant accumulation was forecasted. The women were in the front office of the church waiting for their cue from the ushers after everyone had arrived and been seated. They looked absolutely gorgeous in their dresses, and the jewelry looked exquisite. Bonnie had taken the bridal party to her beauty shop in the mid-afternoon, and Crystal and Maggie had done everyone's hair. One of Cindy's friends who worked for Estée Lauder had applied their makeup, and Lizzy looked like she had just stepped out of *Brides* magazine. Lizzy's something "old" was her engagement ring, her something "new" were the Swarovski earrings, her something "borrowed" was her sister's white pearl necklace, and her something "blue" was her garter.

Brad and the groomsmen waited in the room across the hall, mostly talking about how the Steelers were going to win the Super Bowl this year since Ben Roethlisberger had come back from his injuries. They felt this would be the final showdown between Ben and Tom Brady, who was now playing for the Tampa Buccaneers, and they felt confident Pittsburgh had the championship ring in the bag.

Both the bride, Lizzy, and the groom, Brad, couldn't have been more relaxed. Each of them felt they had truly found their soulmate, and they were so excited about their future together. There was laughter and gaiety in both rooms, and the energy was off the charts.

All the men had red rose boutonnieres on, except Michael and Brad, who wore white. Brad's dad was wearing his long white robe. The women carried bouquets of red roses and baby's breath, except Vickie, who had white roses also mixed in. Lizzy's bouquet was all red roses that had been shaped into a heart.

Vickie had hired a string quartet to play music while the people waited, and also to play the wedding march while Lizzy was coming down the aisle. Close to the time the procession was to begin, Lizzy had a sad moment with Vickie. She told Vickie, fighting back tears so as not to ruin her makeup, "I sure wish Mom and Dad were here. I would have loved to have had Dad walk me down the aisle instead of flying solo. I miss them so much, especially at times like this."

"I miss them, too, but, Lizzy, I think they are here in spirit, so you will be walking down the aisle with him."

They both hugged and adjusted their eye makeup with a tissue.

Then came the knock at the door. It was time. Brad and Brad's dad went down the aisle first, then waited, looking back toward the door, standing in front of the beautifully decorated altar. First down the red carpet aisle runner were Suzie Q and CJ. They met in the middle, locked their arms together, and walked slowly down the runner. Next to come down the aisle were Bonnie and David, followed by Cindy and Vickie's husband, Don. The last couple were Vickie and Michael, followed by Vickie's kids, Colin, standing by his dad with the wedding ring on a red satin heart-shaped pillow. Then Katherine, to stand next to Vickie, went down the aisle, dropping red rose petals along the way.

Then there was a long silence, and the anticipation built for the arrival of the bride. Lizzy took one last deep breath of excitement before she began to walk toward her future, waiting at the end of the aisle. The people all stood and faced her as she passed them. Brad looked at his future wife with such adoration and love, only second to his love of the Lord. He was beaming from ear to ear.

As she stopped at the altar, she gently slid her hand into his, and together they faced Brad's dad. Brad's father began with something all three of them had written: "Brad and Lizzy want to make it clear that they are not here for themselves, but for the One who makes all things possible. They feel they are living proof of God's intervention and want together to strive to fulfill His plans for their lives."

Then he paused and looked at Lizzy. "Lizzy, you need to follow Christ as your spiritual leader first and always fall back on Him like a compass. But you also need to follow Brad, who shares that compass with you. Follow him as your household leader, and listen and respect his decisions."

He took another deep breath and looked at his son. "Brad, you are to love Lizzy as Jesus loves His people, to serve her like Jesus came to serve. For there is one absolute perfect One, Jesus. You both need to understand each other in patience and unconditional forgiveness, which our Lord showed to us."

Brad's dad looked at Lizzy. "Do you, Lizzy, take Brad to be your lawfully wedded husband?"

"Yes."

Brad's dad then looked at Brad. "Do you, Brad, take Lizzy to be your lawfully wedded wife?"

"Yes."

Then Brad's dad said to the congregation, "Does anyone here have reason that these two people should not be joined together? Let him or her speak now." After the silence, Brad's dad quoted Matthew 19:6: "'So, they are no longer two, but one flesh. Therefore, what God has joined together, let no one separate.'"

Brad's father then redirected his attention to Lizzy and told her to repeat after him: "In the presence of God and all these witnesses, I, Lizzy Murphy, take you, Brad Schmidt, to be my beloved husband. To have and to hold you, to honor you, to treasure you, to be at your side in sorrow and joy, in the good times and in the bad times. To love and to cherish you always, and to never give up my faith. I promise you this from my heart, for all the days of my life."

Lizzy repeated the words perfectly as she had memorized them.

Then Brad's dad looked at his son and said, "Repeat after me: In the presence of God and all these witnesses, I, Brad Schmidt, take you, Lizzy Murphy, to be my beloved wife. To have and to hold you, to honor you, to treasure you, to be at your side in sorrow and joy, in the good times and in the bad times. To love and to cherish you always, and to never give up my faith. I promise you this from my heart, for all the days of my life."

Brad, too, repeated the vows perfectly as he had memorized them.

Brad's father then said to Colin, "Hand me the pillow." He took both rings and said to the congregation, "The wedding ring is a symbol of eternity. It is the outward sign of the inward spiritual bond. It's a circular, perpetuated symbol of the endless love that endures forever."

He looked at Lizzy, handed her Brad's ring, and said, "Repeat after me: I, Lizzy, give you, Brad, this ring as the symbol of that endless love that endures forever."

Lizzy repeated the vow and slid Brad's ring onto his left hand, then gave him a wink.

Then he looked at his son and handed him a ring. Brad repeated: "I, Brad, give you, Lizzy, this ring as the symbol of that endless love that endures forever."

Brad repeated the words and slid the ring onto Lizzy's left hand, then he winked back.

Brad and Lizzy went to the altar and lit the unity candle, then knelt and prayed. In unison, they said, "Lord, we come before You to praise Your glorious name. We promise You and everyone here that we will never take our vows for granted. We will live for You together, and we surrender willingly and are forever Yours. In Jesus' name, we pray. Amen."

A song then came over the speakers. They had made it their song: "When God Made You," by Newsong with Natalie Grant. When the last notes of the song faded away, they stood and walked toward the congregation. Brad's dad said, "It is my honor to introduce to you Mr. and Mrs. Bradley Schmidt. Brad, you may kiss the bride."

Brad turned to Lizzy and planted a huge juicy kiss.

The congregation stood with explosive applause as the two walked out of the room.

Teddy made the announcement that anyone who preferred to take the limo or horse and buggy to the reception hall were welcome to do so, while the wedding party took pictures. He reminded them there were limited parking spaces at the pub and that the limos would be running back and forth all night. Tony helped people with their coats and manned the door. Everyone proceeded to what was now known as the Allegheny River Wedding Reception Spot.

CHAPTER 30

Brad, Lizzy, and the wedding party finished taking pictures at the church. The wedding party had already taken the limo down to the reception area while Brad and Lizzy got into the carriage pulled by a white horse.

At first, Brad and Lizzy put the red velvet blanket in the carriage over their legs, but the air was too frigid, so they draped it over their shoulders as the photographer walked alongside snapping pictures. The carriage took a brief intermission to take pictures of them kissing and looking deep into each other's eyes as it headed down Arch Street toward the reception.

When they arrived, everyone was sitting in their assigned seats. The reception hall looked exquisite. The overhead lights had been reduced the perfect amount to allow the incandescent candle centerpieces to fill in the blanks. Lizzy noticed the aroma of the roses and the colors of the poinsettias. Lizzy thought it looked like a picture out of a bridal magazine. She could hardly believe this was all for her and Brad. She was beyond happy.

Everyone stood and clapped as they walked in. They repositioned themselves as the plates of food were delivered by a formal-looking wait staff. Each person received what they had ordered from the selections on the RSVPs they had sent back from the choices of meat: beef Wellington, chicken Kiev, or poached salmon. They could have selected wild rice or sautéed red potatoes, and a choice of either broccoli or asparagus, with or without béarnaise sauce.

Lizzy and Brad sat up front at the wedding party's table, absorbing each moment as they watched the jovial laughter and conversations. The food was perfect, as well as the caterer's service.

Brad's dad stood after the waitstaff had made sure every engraved stemware was filled and proposed a toast.

"First of all, I want to welcome Lizzy to our family. From the brief time we have spent together, I can tell my son made an awesome decision to make you his wife. I have never seen my son so head over heels in love, and I'm glad he finally came to his senses."

The room exploded in laughter.

As he looked at his son, he went on, "In reality, Brad, at this moment I am the proudest father alive. I feel like I am a part of a gold medal Olympic relay team and have just handed the baton to the anchor man. Not only have you sprinted with ease with the church, but you have also become the man any father would be proud to call son. I believe you are going to, with Lizzy's help, finish the race with style and grace, making it to your final destination, heaven."

He lifted his glass. "Here's to you and your beautiful bride. May you live long, healthy lives, always focused on the Lord. I love you both. God bless you."

Brad and Lizzy intertwined their arms with each other as everyone said, "Hear, hear!"

After the libations, Brad and Lizzy walked over to the wedding cake. A spotlight was luminating the beautiful three-tiered cake that Lizzy had made herself. Brad and Lizzy, together with one silver cake-cutting knife with a red satin bow, sliced out a piece of the bottom tier, vanilla cake with roses and buttercream icing. They kissed each other and decided they were going to eliminate the smashing of the cake in each other's faces. Instead, they took a fork and delicately fed each other a bit, then placed a dab of frosting on each other's cheeks instead.

As the cake was cut and distributed to the guests, Lizzy and Brad danced to the song "When God Made You for Me." They both were sad that their parents couldn't be there to do the traditional mother-son and father-daughter dances, but they felt they were there in spirit. They held each other so tightly that they could feel each other's heartbeats.

After the cake plates were removed, the DJ started the music. They had selected mostly upbeat Christian music and then soft, slow-beat Christian music. They had both agreed to throw in some old Motown and top twenty tunes as well. They must have chosen the right music combinations, because the dance floor was packed for several hours.

Brad finally announced that they were going to take a small break to do the ceremonious garter and bouquet throwing.

First, Lizzy sat on a chair in the middle of the dance floor while Brad reached up her dress and dragged down the garter. Lizzy had purposely placed the garter close to her knee for modesty reasons. Brad then propelled it into a crowd of single men. Joe, the musician from the church, must have had rubber-band legs because he snatched it in midair. He then handed it to David Smith, with respect to the injured while on duty veteran. They then saluted each other.

Next, Lizzy turned her back to a group of single girls. It might have seemed orchestrated, but when Lizzy threw the bouquet over her shoulder, like a perfect quarterback pass, it landed squarely in Bonnie's hands.

Lizzy then made an announcement that they were still going to have music for another hour, but they wanted to let people know that the engraved stemware was theirs to keep, and for them to please take a poinsettia home, too.

Just as she looked out through the pub's glass windows, she saw the snow falling on the lit thirty-foot Christmas tree outside on the patio deck. She thought of those words that had been spoken fifty-nine years earlier when the pub opened, which would be apropos to this day: "Like a dream come true," and "a magical day," and "a day to remember."

Just then, Lizzy grabbed Brad and the photographer and dragged them out to the deck. He began taking pictures of them with snow on their hair and eyelashes, with the tree as the backdrop. They were laughing as the snowfall grew heavier, but they laughed even more when they looked around and saw that most of their guests had poured out into the deck as well and were laughing with them, frolicking in the snow.

Brad laughing, yelled, "We really are children of God!"

THE END